The Fullness of Time

The Fullness of Time

JESUS CHRIST, SCIENCE, AND MODERNITY

Kara N. Slade

FOREWORD BY *Willie James Jennings*

CASCADE *Books* · Eugene, Oregon

THE FULLNESS OF TIME
Jesus Christ, Science, and Modernity

Cascade Books
An Imprint of Wipf and Stock Publishers
199 W. 8th Ave., Suite 3
Eugene, OR 97401

www.wipfandstock.com

PAPERBACK ISBN: 978-1-5326-8937-6
HARDCOVER ISBN: 978-1-5326-8938-3
EBOOK ISBN: 978-1-5326-8939-0

Cataloguing-in-Publication data:

Names: Slade, Kara N. | Jennings, Willie James, 1961–, foreword.
Title: The fullness of time : Jesus Christ, science, and modernity / Kara N. Slade ; foreword by Willie James Jennings.
Description: Eugene, OR : Cascade Books, 2021 | Includes bibliographical references and index.
Identifiers: ISBN 978-1-5326-8937-6 (paperback) | ISBN 978-1-5326-8938-3 (hardcover) | ISBN 978-1-5326-8939-0 (ebook)
Subjects: LCSH: Time—Religious aspects—Christianity. | God (Christianity)—Eternity.
Classification: BT78 .S48 2021 (print) | BT78 .S48 (ebook)

To the greater glory of God
and in loving memory of Philip Earl Slade, Jr.

I know that my Redeemer liveth, and that he shall stand at the latter day upon the earth; and though this body be destroyed, yet shall I see God; whom I shall see for myself and mine eyes shall behold, and not as a stranger.[1]

1. *Book of Common Prayer 1979*, 469.

Contents

CONTENTS

Foreword

WILLIE JAMES JENNINGS

This is hard time. Many people feel it. They know it in their bodies. They sense a duration that somehow, inexplicably, has become demonically controlled. It is a duration that first plots them temporally—they are either underdeveloped or developed and if those positions do not quite capture them, then they are outside history itself, clearly unseen even in being seen. Those fortunate enough to be seen in this time, let us call it unredeemed time, even demonically controlled time, are then invited to marvel at cosmic time and enter the one true and decisive story of their origins. But this is not a story told by one's parents or one's people or formed through faiths that form life and chart good living. This story of your origins is imperial, created by the one for the many. The one—let us, following the author of this book, call him scientific man—quickly and quietly silenced your parents, your people, and your faith. He told them that they may speak after he has spoken and in that *after* they will learn their place. It is not a pedagogical place, not a place of knowing and insight. It will be a place of inspiration, like a dessert served after the main course of which one may decide not to partake after becoming full of the substantive main course. Scientific man will be loving and kind as long as everyone keeps their place, but as soon as any people or religion or person dares to question his telling, question his story, he then reveals the power he claims but has not yet fully achieved. It is the power to close the gap between his story, his telling, and history itself, and the power to close the gap between his stage name "scientific man" and science itself.

This is his time, which is a usurpation of our time. He in his time desires to tell us how we should live in time, how to count our days, how and where to place value, significance, and most importantly purpose. He wants to give us purpose-driven time. Yet he beautifully hides his adversarial position by performing a strange sort of humility that tells us that what we might become together through time is completely in our hands. "It is all up to us," he says. But so many people understand that it is in fact not up to us, because the "us" has already been delimited to those who have achieved development, having distinguished themselves from those lagging behind and those who have not even begun to walk the path toward the light of modern time. Yet for those who have accepted his time as their time, all that remains is the struggle to make sense of this time. We must work while we have the light of day and the light of night. Unfortunately, the combination of these lights too often robs us of the difference between day and night and the necessary rhythms of rest and work. More importantly, they rob us of even knowing what work and rest should look like. This is time that has fallen into our hands and thereby become unbearably heavy like a weight no human being should ever try to carry alone or collectively.

How is it possible that we have come to believe that we have the strength to carry time, master it with the same ambition that gave shape to modern colonial slavery? That belief forms inside another belief—that somehow through the cunning of reason and the power of our technology, we are outside time, beholding it like gods from all eternity—charting periods, epochs, moments, highs and lows, advancement, regression. The particularly peculiar history of European man with the emergence of whiteness situates this effect of modernity—time deformed and deforming.

Kara Slade courageously challenges deformed and deforming time. This is not an easy task, because to question time in the way she does in this book makes her susceptible to being misinterpreted by those who do not grasp a basic theological axiom: time is a creature. Time had a beginning and it will have an ending. Thus, time itself cannot be the container of all beginnings and endings. Those who make time the container will inevitably become confused with their own sense of agency. They will think they can master time—ride it like a surfer rides a wave—or they will think that there is no hope of its mastery and therefore they are resolved to simply float along its currents hoping for the best while trying not to drown. Kara Slade aims to help us understand our agency in time by understanding time as a gift given not by scientific man or his European father but by God. As

Karl Barth taught us, time is God's eternity loaned to the creature. We have, however, badly handled time. Thus, an intervention was necessary.

Dr. Slade reflects on that divine intervention that goes by the name Jesus Christ and in so doing intervenes in one of the crucial problems of scientific modernity—its colonial, imperialist, racist deployment of time. She is uniquely equipped to do this emergency work being trained as a scientist, a theologian, and a priest. She understands the mystifications that happen when Christians and their theologians say the word "science." Its utterance conjures an intellectual citadel filled with knowledge and knowers and institutions and projects and resources and wealth and power and prestige all lumped together inside walls that separate them from us mere non-scientists. Slade will have none of this dangerous foolishness. Science means people using various methods to understand things. Science means people who are sinners saved by grace using various methods to understand things. Science means people who are sinners saved by grace using various methods that have an uneven history of being helpful or harmful, having been formed and yet being formed inside colonialist and imperialist histories that influence how we understand things. Science means people who are sinners saved by grace using various methods that have an uneven history of being helpful or harmful, having been formed and yet being formed inside colonialist and imperialist histories that influence how we destroy or create, forget or remember, misinterpret or understand forms of life and ways of living. In short, science is a work of the creature and must, as she argues in this book, be thought through a creaturely theology.

Twenty-first-century scientific modernity pathologizes people who refuse its alchemy of time. Sadly, too many Christians have accepted its diagnoses and have thereby yielded to the real pathologies of our time. This means that the serious work that must yet be done is convincing Christians that they do in fact live in a different time, that is, the actual time bound up in God's eternity. We live from the middle having our beginning and our ending brought to us through Jesus Christ. This is the insight of Dietrich Bonhoeffer. We touch time, our hands freed from the illusion that we carry it, knowing that God holds time, graciously keeping it from collapsing back into the nothingness out of which it came. Touching time for us means grace, always grace in which we live in the *exitus et reditus*, the going from and the returning to God. Slade invites us in this powerful reflection on time to deepen our liturgical awareness of time that is not simply the wisdom of how to live but an insight into actual life: We are in God's time that is also our time.

A word needs to be said, finally, about the loss of time. So many people are being robbed of time now not only in the sense of being cursed with this demonically influential vision of time, with its deep pathologies, but also robbed through the deployment of this vision of time in the ways modern nation-states and modern corporations calculate value, worth, and work. Time is increasingly drained of all meaning and joy, squeezed as we are between the state and the corporation and their shared project of monetizing our every motion, weaving us all into their hoped-for eternal cycle of producer to consumer to producer and back to consumer, a demonic *exitus et reditus* that is not earth-bound as much as it is death-bound. If ever we will break with this time and enter redeemed time, thereby redeeming our time, it will take many more works like this one. Thankfully, we have this book to begin us.

Willie James Jennings
New Haven, Connecticut

Acknowledgments

B oth priesthood and scholarship are communal endeavors. The work of theology in and for the sake of the church cannot be done without others. There are so many people to whom I owe so much, and for whom these "private words addressed in public" (in the words of T. S. Eliot) can only stand as a token down payment.

It is difficult to find the words to express my gratitude to my mentors in this work, especially to Willie James Jennings and Amy Laura Hall. Since the fall of 2010, when their teaching changed my life and revitalized my faith, they have walked with me, encouraged me, and pushed me to ask deeper and more faithful questions. I am proud to be their student, and proud to take my place in the lineage of Lindbeck, Outka, and Wainwright. Thanks to J. Kameron Carter for pushing me to ask deeper questions, to Rey Chow for teaching me how to read Foucault, and to Gerald McKenny for supporting my work with warmth and friendship, even from afar.

I am grateful as well for the material support that made my research possible, including funding from the Graduate School of Duke University, the Graduate Program in Religion, Duke Divinity School, and the Kearns Foundation. Special thanks are due to Stephen Chapman and Carol Rush of the GPR for helping me over all the administrative hurdles. Angela Rayner inspired the introduction by showing me the Chronophage during a visit to Cambridge. Duke Divinity School, Perkins Library, and Trinity Church Princeton provided the physical and mental space to write. Meghan Florian edited the manuscript for submission, and without her help I could not have finished in a timely manner.

The people of Church of the Nativity, St. Paul's, St. Stephen's, and St. David's parishes, as well as the Anglican and Episcopal students at Duke Divinity School, have been infinitely patient with me as I have learned how

to be a priest. My mentors and friends in the church, in Durham and beyond, have made all the difference in who I have become, especially Bishops
Philip Duncan, Michael Curry, Anne Hodges-Copple, and Sam Rodman,
along with Thack Dyson, David Marshall, Ellen Davis, Stanley Hauerwas,
Joe Carnes Ananias, Stephanie Allen, Rhonda Mawhood Lee, and Clarke
and Sally French.

While this project started in Durham, it is ending in Princeton. So
many encouragers and companions have come alongside me in the final
miles of this marathon. Bishop Chip Stokes and the staff of the Diocese of
New Jersey have welcomed this Southerner and made me feel part of the
family. To the people of Trinity Church, and to my colleagues Paul Jeanes,
Joanne Epply-Schmidt, Chris McNabb, and Tom Whittemore: thank you.
Following Jesus alongside you continues to be a gift. My Daily Office companions have kept me accountable to the rhythms of the Daily Office, particularly the students of Princeton Seminary. The Center for Barth Studies
has changed the trajectory of my career with its conferences and colloquia
for advanced doctoral students. Special thanks are due to my fellow scholar-
priest, Sonia Waters of Princeton Seminary, for her constant good humor
and friendship. Thanks are also due to Joseph Wolyniak for supporting
the work of scholar-priests like me in a multitude of ways throughout the
years, not least by making it possible for me to live out my vocation in this
community.

I am grateful to my mother, Nancy Slade, for her love and patience as
I completed my second doctorate. I know she is relieved that I finally have a
proper job. Finally, I acknowledge the one to whom I stand in infinite debt,
and in whose service I have pledged myself and my life's work:

> Were the whole realm of nature mine,
> That were an offering far too small;
> Love so amazing, so divine,
> Demands my soul, my life, my all.[2]

As I write these words on St. Anselm's Day, I pray the blessings
of the Triune God on all who will read this attempt at "faith seeking
understanding."

Princeton, New Jersey
Feast of St. Anselm of Canterbury
April 21, 2018

2. Isaac Watts, "When I Survey the Wondrous Cross," *The Hymnal 1982* (New York: Church Hymnal Corporation, 1985) 474.

1

Introduction

Let me know you, O you who know me; then shall I know even as I am known. You are the strength of my soul; make your way in and shape it to yourself, that it may be yours to have and to hold, free from stain or wrinkle. I speak because this is my hope, and whenever my joy springs from that hope it is joy well founded. As for the rest of this life's experiences, the more tears are shed over them the less are they worth weeping over, and the more truly worth lamenting the less do we bewail them while mired in them. You love the truth because anyone who does truth comes to the light. Truth it is that I want to do, in my heart by confession in your presence, and with my pen before many witnesses.

—ST. AUGUSTINE OF HIPPO[1]

A pamphlet writer such as I am has no seriousness, as you presumably will hear about me—why, then, should I now in conclusion pretend seriousness in order to please people by making a rather big promise? In other words, to write a pamphlet is frivolity—but to promise the system, that is seriousness and has made many a man a supremely serious man both in his own eyes and in the eyes of others.

—SØREN KIERKEGAARD[2]

1. Augustine, *Confessions*, 197.
2. Kierkegaard, *Philosophical Fragments*, 109.

On September 19, 2008, between the feasts of the Holy Cross and St. Matthew the Evangelist by the liturgical calendar, Stephen Hawking unveiled the Chronophage, a new public clock built by inventor John Taylor for Corpus Christi College, Cambridge. Its mechanism features a large mechanical grasshopper and an irregular movement, designed to impress upon passersby the unpredictability and terror of human existence in time. Taylor describes his creation in colorful terms:

> The Chronophage Clock's pendulum slows down, speeds up and even stops, with the time shown by lights racing around the face. The time is exactly correct every fifth minute to one hundredth of a second. Time is not on your side, it's rather scary, so with the Corpus Chronophage I changed the cuddly image of a Walt Disney grasshopper into a rather frightening time eater. I thought it would be fun if in a minute he slowly opened his jaws wider and wider, and on the 59th second of every minute he went crunch, got that minute, chewed it up and swallowed it so you could never get it back.[3]

The clock's effect, which, according to Taylor, is "meant" to be "terrifying," is further intensified by the sound of a chain dropped into a small wooden coffin to chime the hour, as well as the biblical quotation from the Vulgate that appears below it.[4] The excerpt is from 1 John 2:17, translated in English as "the world and its desire are passing away." Tellingly, though, the second half of the verse is omitted. In its entirety, 1 John 2:17 reads, "And the world and its desire are passing away, but those who do the will of God live forever."[5]

While preparing the final manuscript of this book for publication, I stumbled upon a blog post from the BioLogos Institute—ironically also entitled "The Fullness of Time"—that discussed the Chronophage as a site of theological reflection. The BioLogos editors contend that the clock offers Christians a "gift towards humility" and a "reminder that time is a gift."[6] On the contrary, I believe that the Chronophage marks time according to the secular liturgies of twenty-first-century scientific modernity. Inaugurated by a luminary of unquestioned scientific authority, it teaches people and forms them in the belief that time is a threat and that death is final.[7]

3. Taylor, "Chronophage," para. 6.

4. Kennedy, "Beware the Time-Eater."

5. 1 John 2:17 (NRSV).

6. Biologos Institute, "Fullness of Time," para. 9.

7. Taylor, "Chronophage."

Even the carefully edited Scripture passage that appears beneath it has been shorn of any hope. Ironically, its location and its name bear a hint of the older, Christian liturgical time it tries to supplant: Corpus Christi, the medieval feast that commemorates the institution of the Eucharist and the real presence of Christ in the sacrament of Communion. There, on a street corner in Cambridge, two narratives of time collide. That collision is the focus of this book.

Preliminary Expectorations

Everything that follows depends upon a theological assertion in which God is the acting subject. The Triune God has acted, acts, and will act freely in loving relationship to the created world in and through the covenant of grace. In Jesus Christ, the eternal God took on human temporality. The creator irrupted into created time. In doing so, God embraced, redeemed, and liberated human existence in time.

As part of dogmatic reflection on the God-world relationship, a Christian account of time belongs within the doctrine of creation. Unfortunately, Christian theological writing on time has, for the most part, proceeded by way of abstract speculation, or worked towards a seamless harmonization of modern science and theology that often creates more problems than it solves. At its core, this book is an attempt to take the summons to creaturely theology seriously, and to do theology as a creature relating to the Creator as revealed in Jesus Christ. It does not intend to deliver an encyclopedic theology of time and history. It does not, in the words of Søren Kierkegaard quoted in the epigraph, "promise the system."[8] Instead, it presents a series of examples that illustrate how scientific modernity shapes our assumptions about time, with pressing dogmatic and moral implications for the proclamation and witness of the church in the late-capitalist West. Rather than present a comprehensive survey of Christian theologies of time, it attends closely to the work of Søren Kierkegaard and Karl Barth, two thinkers who saw clearly the presenting issues of their age and offered a theological alternative that was neither a flight into nostalgia nor an uncritical embrace of modern thought.

What might a Christian account of created time and creaturely life in that time look like? Augustine's reflection on time in the *Confessions* grew out of an exegesis of "In the beginning, God created . . . ," and to be sure that has been a consistent pattern in the Christian tradition. Where else can

8. Kierkegaard, *Philosophical Fragments*, 109.

we begin but the beginning, even as that beginning constantly tempts us to secure our own position by thinking behind it—by attempting to think ourselves into eternity? As Dietrich Bonhoeffer noted in his own exegesis of Genesis 1, human thought "pounds itself to pieces" on a beginning that it both "wants and cannot want power to attain."[9] Bonhoeffer explains that the Christian life in time is not a matter of securing the beginning but of living from the middle, having received both the beginning and end from Christ—and only from Christ. What Bonhoeffer covered in a few pages in 1933, Karl Barth would explore more than a decade later in all its implications. Strikingly, and characteristically, Barth's argument in *Church Dogmatics* III/2 from Jesus as the Lord of Time to creaturely life in time hinges on a different passage entirely. He reasons not from the beginning, but from the constancy and contemporaneity of Jesus Christ in Hebrews 13:8: "Jesus Christ the same yesterday, today, and forever."

The result is not just christological as a form of window dressing, proceeding with an argument from creation that notes in passing the participation of the Word in that creation. Instead, Barth's logic is christological all the way down, and as such it shows what it means to confess in the creed that "through him all things were made" as the external basis of the covenant of grace. This is an account of time that contradicts the human belief that our time—past, present, and future—is either ultimately about us, or it is about nothing. It leaves no room for faith in human progress, but at the same time it leaves no room for despair. While it is a contradiction, it is the contradiction of grace and liberation, embrace and gift.

This emphasis on Christ's presence with us here in the middle of our times, from the "moment" of the saving encounter with Christ and the call to discipleship and witness, is a theological theme that reflects the deep influence of Kierkegaard on both Bonhoeffer and Barth. While Barth distanced himself from Kierkegaard in some aspects of his later work, he also denied he had left Kierkegaard behind entirely. As he noted in an address in 1963,

> [Kierkegaard] became one of the cocks whose crowing seemed to proclaim from near and far the dawn of a really new day. . . . There were to be for all of us, and indeed especially for me, new dawns with new questions and answers, and yet I believe that throughout my theological life I have remained faithful to Kierkegaard's *reveille* as we heard it then, and that I am still faithful to it today. Going back to Hegel . . . has been out of the question ever since.[10]

9. Bonhoeffer, *Creation and Fall*, 26.
10. Barth, "Thank-You and a Bow," 97.

This book will read Kierkegaard alongside Barth, but not with the goal of tracing lines of influence in the history of ideas or solving the question of the relationship between the two thinkers. Instead, I hope to highlight the ways both figures rejected an approach to time that was, and is, not coincidentally intertwined with a racialized account of history and the co-opting of Christianity by the modern Western state.

Methodology

While I will describe how human existence in time is determined by the time of Jesus Christ, by the logic of the incarnation, passion, resurrection, and ascension, the predominant accounts of time in the modern West have proceeded from a very different basis. These approaches have implications not just for epistemology, and they are not only a matter of accepting or rejecting abstract doctrinal and philosophical claims. They have had, and continue to have, concrete effects on human life together. They have often been death-dealing rather than life-giving, marked by a series of moral errors this project hopes to interrupt. In the words of historian Jenny Reardon, they participate at the deepest level in one of the key features of modernity: "the entanglement of rules that govern what can count as knowledge with rules that determine which human lives can be lived."[11] In short, the logic of scientific modernity has features that make time a stage for agonism and violence instead of love and redemption.

I write from within an Anglican tradition that has historically been all too ready to participate in that logic—to deploy its authority to support colonial domination, the slave trade, and the eugenics movement. But I do so as a priest as well as a scholar, and I do so with the hope that this book can offer Anglicans another way forward in repentance and in hope. My work is above all an exercise of my priesthood, and it does not aspire to significance for its own sake—or for mine.

This book also marks an intentional divergence from a set of unhelpful conversations that too often have captured the conversations it engages. These conversations usually travel under the category of "science and religion." Unlike most of the often well-funded and heavily promoted scholarship in this field, this project does not attempt to fashion a coherent account of scientific knowledge and the contested category of religion as a general concept. It is grounded in Christian particularity rather than the category of religion, works in the register of ethics rather than epistemology, and

11. Reardon, *Race to the Finish*, 5.

casts a critical eye on the idea of "science" as a monolithic, universal, and ahistorical entity.

In a 2011 essay commemorating the full communion agreement between the Episcopal Church and the ELCA, William Danaher noted the significant gifts that Anglican moral theology could receive from Lutheranism. Danaher describes a contemporary Anglican consensus that has yet to grapple with its own legacy of colonialism, is often blind to its own cultural assimilation, and overemphasizes sacramentality and the incarnation in ways that can underwrite the political and social status quo. He suggests the classic Lutheran emphases on the theology of the cross, on the logic of redemption rather than incarnation, and on the importance of the proclaimed word might serve as a much-needed corrective for Anglican theology.[12]

This ecumenical approach has motivated my own desire to read Kierkegaard alongside Barth as an Anglican theologian. While this book is, above all, a study of primary theological texts, it also incorporates other sources in two ways. First, it draws on history and contemporary culture for concrete examples of particular patterns of rhetoric and thought. The examples in this book are not meant to be exhaustive, and they are by no means the only ones I could have used. They are used for illustrative rather than encyclopedic purposes. Second, just as Barth used secular philosophy on an *ad hoc* basis for theological purposes, this project uses critical and theoretical insights in the same way. A reading of critical theory may indeed be helpful for practical reasoning, even if it is in no way determinative for theology.

Chapter Outline

There are four chapters to this book, each of which is focused on a different temporal problem. They begin with examples that illustrate the problem under consideration. Then, they move through a discussion of how the person and work of Jesus Christ, read through the work of Kierkegaard and Barth, might offer a different vision for the church—a new possibility for both seeing and living. Each chapter ends with a reflection on liturgical time that corresponds to its theological focus: Passiontide and Easter, Advent, Christmas, and finally Ascensiontide and Pentecost, before concluding with ordinary time. Not only do the chapters correspond to liturgical

12. Danaher, "Renewing the Anglican Moral Vision."

seasons, but they also trace the trajectory of the Christian life, as Barth does, from Baptism to Eucharist, from death and resurrection in Christ to the means of grace that sustain Christian life together.

In deploying this liturgical structure, I do not mean to suggest the observance of the church year somehow solves the deeply entrenched problems described herein. Neither do I mean to suggest, for example, the matter of endings is only related to Advent. Rather, I hope to use these events as focal points for reflecting on the relationship between God's saving work and our own witness in our time.

The first chapter addresses the question of origins, and of the self-narrating self that is generated by it. It opens with the example of Big History, and the convergence of scientific authority with the mystification and fascination that the temporal origin represents. It then turns to a theoretical consideration of this convergence, examining in particular the connection between Denise Ferreira da Silva's two forms of modern humanity as it is generated by modern thought: the Hegelian and the Darwinian. Then, the chapter turns to readings of Kierkegaard and Barth that may be helpful in interpreting and critiquing modern, scientific accounts of the beginning. In the works of Kierkegaard, both *Johannes Climacus* and *Philosophical Fragments* are helpful critiques of the attempt to secure a beginning for human thought. Similarly, for Barth, the paschal event of cross and resurrection is the only allowable starting point for dogmatic reflection on creaturely time. By developing his account of human temporality in *Church Dogmatics* III/2 from Hebrews 13:8 instead of Genesis 1, Barth reorients the question of human origins to Christ, rather than to the easily co-opted creation at the beginning of time.

By claiming the time of Jesus as "at once the centre and the beginning and the end of all the lifetimes of all," Barth shifts the vexatious conversation between theology and science that often centers on questions of origins to a much more fertile and congenial ground, away from either the collision or convergence of worldviews and towards witness to the risen Lord.[13] Consequently, the guiding liturgical focus for this chapter is Passiontide and Easter. The starting point for theological engagements with time, and for this book, is the saving event by which God in Christ triumphed over sin and death.

The question of beginnings is intimately tied to the question of endings or eschatologies, and it is to the latter topic that the next chapter turns.

13. Barth, *Church Dogmatics* III/2, 440.

Human efforts to secure their own beginning are deeply intertwined with efforts to bring about a particular vision of the end. Here, my concern is two-fold. First, this chapter addresses progressive, postmillennial eschatologies that elide or erase particular human beings in a vision of cosmic progress. It is also concerned with technological utopianism as well as collectivist forms of reactionary thought that have influenced contemporary American politics. Some of these projects share a vision of time as an ever-ascending trajectory of human progress and technological self-mastery, even though they differ on the possibilities of moral progress. Others embrace a cyclical temporal model in which the life of the national social body must be periodically purged and renewed through shared, collective sacrifice.

After considering the past and the future, the third chapter turns to the present, and specifically to the ways some people are marked as existing in the present, while others are described as variously regressive or outside of history. This tactic carries with it a politics that often is racialized, mixed with discourses of civilization and primitivity, in present-day America as well as in historical contexts. Johannes Fabian's concepts of temporal distancing and coeval status can provide an analytic tool to describe this temporal pathology incisively. Theologically, the phenomenon of temporal distancing poses the question of the neighbor, that is: Who is the neighbor, and what is the language that marks some people as outside the category of neighbor?

The fourth and final chapter builds on the previous three. Its topic is the intellectual move outside of time in order to evaluate either our time or a previous time. From this vantage point, the form of the "fullness of time" is determined, and the time of the neighbor may also be determined, managed, and controlled. Theoretically, this maneuver is related to what Denise Ferreira da Silva calls the position of transparency to reason. This position exists over and against the position of affectability insofar as the one assuming it presupposes they are always, already outside of the laws of nature.

Rather than place ourselves outside of time in order to evaluate and control it, our time is redeemed and given to us in Christ—who, as Barth notes, is in his person the fullness of time. The risen and ascended Christ counters the logic of achieving self-ascension by force, by catapulting oneself outside of time. Finally, the ascension is tied closely to the sending of the Holy Spirit at Pentecost and the gift of that Spirit to the church. At the event of Pentecost, this work finally turns to matters of ordinary, Spirit-filled Christian life in ordinary time.

2

Beginnings

God creates out of nothing—marvelous, you say. Yes, of course, but he does something more marvelous: he creates saints out of sinners.

—SØREN KIERKEGAARD[1]

Jesus Christ is the same yesterday and today and forever.

—HEBREWS 13:8 (NRSV)

Let me tell you a story. We learn through childhood experience that proper stories begin with "once upon a time," but that is not how this story begins. Instead, it begins in the middle, with two examples from seemingly disparate ends of contemporary culture. The first is the Terrence Malick film *The Tree of Life* (2011), much beloved by many young Christians in the United States. In its opening seconds, a placard flashes on the screen with the familiar words of Job 38:4, 7: "Where were you when I laid the earth's foundation . . . while the morning stars sang together and all the sons of God shouted for joy?" Soon after, the viewer is immersed in an extended visual meditation on those words, an attempt to imagine what it might have been like to be there when the foundations of the universe were laid. The cosmos takes shape, from formless void to stars and galaxies. The Milky

---

1. Kierkegaard, *Søren Kierkegaard's Journals and Papers*, vol. 2, II A 758 n.d. 1838.

Way coalesces into being. Meanwhile, a version of the *Lacrimosa* from the Requiem Mass is played while a woman's voice intones:

> Where were you?
> Did you know?
> Who are we to you?
> Answer me.[2]

As it continues, the film intersperses scenes of the protagonist's family life in Texas with a vision of creation in which God is a distant, utterly transcendent Other. God's question to Job, "Where were you?," is reflected back on a God who is alluded to only as a distant, and seemingly cold, fire at the heart of all that is.

Malick's 2011 effort was followed in 2016 by *Voyage of Time*, an exploration and expansion of the same temporal and religious themes that made their debut in *Tree of Life*. Again, the particularity of the God of Israel who spoke to Job is replaced by a universalized impetus to love, to know, and to shape the world that human beings have been given. As reviewer Richard Brody writes in the *New Yorker*,

> For Malick, this vision of a universal consciousness, the reflection of something like the mind in all existence, is the very basis for science—including social science—as well as of art. The core of "Voyage of Time" is the search for a beginning, for the emotional and aesthetic energy that gives rise to the scientific and artistic impulses, the urge for discovery and creation. In effect, that energy, if it exists, would be a kind of love—a generalized precursor to divine love that owes nothing to organized religion but suggests passionate affinities, rather than oppressive constraints, grand connections that aren't empathetic but aesthetic. The drive to comprehend the world, to explore it, to depict it, and to improve it are presented here as inseparable.[3]

Brody continues with a cautionary, parenthetical note: "Whether his vision is an accurate depiction of the natural world or an aspirational one is another story altogether."[4] Whether or not one subscribes to Malick's artistic vision, the fact that he seemed compelled to return to these themes in 2016 is diagnostic of the cultural moment. What he explored aesthetically in a film that comparatively few will ever see is also the subject matter of a

---

2. Malick, *Tree of Life*, 20:05.
3. Brody, "Terrence Malick's Metaphysical Journey into Nature," para. 8.
4. Brody, "Terrence Malick's Metaphysical Journey into Nature," para. 8.

pedagogical project for a much broader audience: a scientific approach to the teaching of history in K-12 education in the United States. That is the subject of the second example, and where this work begins in earnest.

Big History, Trowels, and Backhoes

The educational movement that would later become known as the Big History Project began unassumingly, with an article in the *Journal of World History* by Australian scholar David Christian. Christian's "Case for 'Big History'" argued that the "appropriate time scale" for scholarship and the teaching of history is not the time scale of a human lifetime, but rather "the whole of time."[5] His reasons for this approach are both philosophical and political. First, as he explains, "big history permits the asking of very large questions and therefore encourages the search for larger meanings in the past."[6] In this way, big history "encourages us to ask questions about our place in the universe," and "leads us back to the sort of questions that have been answered in many societies by creation myths."[7] First, and most importantly, the project is centered on an account of human meaning that is grounded in the authority of scientific objectivity. Second, Christian hoped to prompt a political discussion of the role of growth and progress that he believed had been obscured by teaching of history on smaller, human scales. Whatever nuance Christian originally hoped to add to this consideration of progress, however, would be lost in the popularization of his work in a TED talk 20 years later.

Christian would rise to public prominence in the wake of that 2011 lecture, in which he presented his case for Big History to the technocapitalists of Silicon Valley. Among that audience was Bill Gates, who became enamored with Big History's scientific framing of contemporary humanity's origin story.[8] In the wake of that event, the Big History Project became a slickly packaged, Gates Foundation–funded effort to bring its sweeping account of time and its "framework for all knowledge" to elementary and

5. Christian, "Case for 'Big History,'" 223.

6. Christian, "Case for 'Big History,'" 227.

7. Christian, "Case for 'Big History,'" 227.

8. It should be noted that Christian's TED talk and the release of *The Tree of Life* took place in the same year.

secondary schools. It has been supplemented by a proliferation of academic and popular texts, as well as with its own journal.[9]

The scientific metanarrative of Big History traces a story of development through eight threshold or transition points that function as the keys to understanding the past, present, and future. The first five are the unremarkable subject matter of eighth-grade science classes: the Big Bang, the emergence of stars, the proliferation of chemical elements, the beginnings of earth and the solar system, and the first organic life on earth. Only in the last three do human beings enter the picture. The past, present, and future of human life is encompassed and determined by three transition points: collective learning, agriculture, and the emergence of a globalized industrial modernity. The latter is described in a manner that transforms an act of politics and economics into an act of nature:

> When humans began to take advantage of advances in transportation, exploring unknown parts of the world, they ushered in an exchange of people, ideas, plants, animals, and diseases among formerly separate regions. By the early nineteenth century three factors—the interconnected world zones, the expansion and the importance of commerce, and the discovery of fossil fuels—began to rapidly transform some societies. Several of these regions found their wealth and power grew at an enormous rate, setting the stage for the first truly modern societies.[10]

The pedagogical and political effect of such an account is clear, marking the political and economic status quo, along with its history, as natural and inevitable in precisely the same way as the emergence of chemical elements.

The narrative of Big History explicitly describes itself as a secular, scientific, and objective origin story and a source of meaning intended to complement, if not to replace, that of the Christian story. It is a doctrine of creation for those who have progressed beyond creatureliness, where providence unfolds in the spread of globalized capitalism. In the words of the project website, "Since the earliest humans, we've struggled to make sense of our world and understand where we come from. Big History, which presents a perspective based on modern science, is simply another attempt to answer the big questions about our beginnings."[11] At first

9. See, for example, Christian, *Maps of Time*; Brown, *Big History*; and *The Journal of Big History*, whose first issue was published in January 2017.

10. "Crisscrossing and Connected," Subheading 4.

11. "Big History Teaching Guide," 7.

glance, such an effort might seem harmless enough. It may appear to be the latest instantiation of what conservative religious commentators might call a product of secularization, or evidence of an age that believes it can do without God. To understand what precisely is wrong with such a project, however, it is necessary to think outside the binaries left over from the fundamentalist-modernist controversy. The problem is not that Big History can do without God. The problem of Big History, along with similar projects to scientifically narrate human origins, is the way its theoretical basis travels into theological thought.

The first difficulty with this account has already been alluded to. The metanarrative presented by Big History, especially in its popularized forms, downplays or ignores the role of racialized colonialism in favor of a unified narrative of the unfolding of globalization. However, this problem does not exist in isolation. One of the key contentions of this book is that the role of race in scientific metanarratives like Big History is enmeshed at the deepest level with its appeal to scientific authority and its inhuman time scale, marking some human beings as the victors of history and others as its dross.

The role of scientific authority, especially as it places particular people at the apex of reason, also undergirds Big History and its philosophical kin. Claims to scientific authority, and claims by scientific figures who are seen as authoritative, can take on the significance of priestly proclamation. The effects of this appeal to authority can be seen in venues that range from the aforementioned works on human origins to articles in the popular press that breathlessly report the latest findings of neuroscience or the latest evolutionary explanation for modern Western social behavior.

Finally, scientific authority, or what Denise Ferreira da Silva calls the figure of scientific man, also occupies a particular place at the apex of a temporal trajectory of progress.[12] From this vantage point, scientific man is able to catapult himself outside of time to envision time and history on the most massive, Hegelian scale. From there, the authority of science and of scientific man is deployed to arrange other human beings on a developmental scale of primitivism and progress. Actual human beings, existing at the time scale of a human life, disappear and can too easily be disregarded through this procedure.

To the extent that Christians have engaged with this project, they have predictably done so in ways that remain captive to the terms of the

---

12. Ferreira da Silva, *Toward a Global Idea of Race*, 113.

fundamentalist-modernist controversy, and to the assumption that epistemology is the only ground of contention that matters in the relationship between science and Christian faith. One recent engagement with Big History
has come from Catholic theologian John Haught, for whom Big History
represents "a sacramental opening" that renews "our sense of the infinity
and personality of God." Blending the thought of David Christian with that
of Pierre Teilhard de Chardin, Haught suggests a Christian "metaphysics
of the future" could incorporate "the realities of evolutionary struggle, in-
nocent suffering, and moral evil" as regrettable but acceptable casualties of
the great process of cosmic becoming.[13]

For Ted Peters, the perspective of Big History is problematic only insofar as subjectivity is hidden within the story it tells. He writes,

> Any story of nature's history told strictly from within the scien-
> tific gaze requires an objectivist or third person perspective. . . .
> Now, please do not mistake me. I celebrate the scientific gaze. This
> third person gaze has proved to be of inestimable value during
> the rise of the natural sciences in the modern West. Restricting
> itself to empirical research and rational reflection, the scientific
> method has demonstrated its fruitfulness beyond measure. Scien-
> tific research is progressive, leading daily to new discoveries and
> new knowledge. Modern civilization can only say "thank you" to
> our scientific method and to the energy of the devoted research-
> ers among us. The price paid for this scientific advance, however,
> has been the sacrifice of meaning and the game of pretend that
> says subjectivity does not count in human knowing. We discover
> this when we shuffle our theological trowel below the soil surface.
> Here, we uncover an enormously influential assumption at work
> in modern science, namely, the exclusion of mind, consciousness,
> personhood, and, therefore, meaning.[14]

For Peters, a little "shuffling of the theological trowel" is needed to "dig
around" and "expose" the "existential questions" that "are already buried
within scientific accounts of our cosmos and the evolution of life."[15] But
Peters's Tillichian solution is to dig under the surface to uncover a substrate
of true and universal meaning that is already there. On the other hand,
this book assumes a backhoe, and not a trowel, is needed to excavate what

---

13. Haught, "Big History, Scientific Naturalism, and Christian Hope," 80.

14. Peters, "Big History and Big Questions," 56–57.

15. Peters, "Big History and Big Questions," 48.

lies under, behind, and beneath the accounts of Big History and similar projects.

The methodology of the Big History project itself, with its underlying philosophy of "Universal Darwinism," is only one of the most visible, and most easily unpacked, examples of an impulse that can be seen in the Malick films with which this chapter began. It is also an impulse that can be seen in contemporary theological projects that range from the evangelical BioLogos foundation, supported by former NIH director Francis Collins, to the liberal Protestant-Unitarian vision of Michael Dowd's *The Great Story* project.[16] Each of these examples assumes that the story that tells us who we are, where we have come from, and where we are going as human beings is the story of the beginning: the beginning of time, the beginning of the material universe, and the beginning of the human species. Only by grasping the story of the beginning, so the argument goes, can we understand the story we inhabit now. As a result, the relationship of science and theology is framed in terms that almost inevitably lead to theology's mystification by scientific claims of objectivity and authority. Also as a result, theology responds anxiously to create a seamlessly coherent account of that beginning. Theology assumes a defensive posture that strives to make contemporary cosmology, evolutionary biology, and Christian doctrine cohere with each other in an encyclopedic vision of all that is and all that has been. In order to offer an alternate constructive account, I turn first to the theoretical backhoe work that can help us uncover the moral problems raised by both the baptized and secular versions of Big History, as well as other scientific origin stories. That work begins with the masculine figure of the scientist, or "scientific man," upon whose authority those stories depend.

Homo Scientificus and the Transparent "I"

Who is this figure of scientific man? How does this figure embody the self-narrating, self-generating human? How does a scientific story of origins become the determinative story of humanity that describes humanity's purpose? One starting point in answering these questions is to examine how "scientific man" emerged as a paradigmatic figure in the eighteenth and nineteenth centuries, and how that emergence was tied to a particular,

16. See, for example, their respective websites at http://biologos.org/about-us/ and http://thegreatstory.org/home.html.

heroic portrayal of the scientist and the concept of scientific objectivity as heroic labor.

In one account, Mary Terrall describes the emergence of the heroic narrative in early scientific historiography, as well as the patterns it set for the public image of scientists and science as a monolithic entity. She traces this trajectory at least to early descriptions of Isaac Newton, and especially to Nicolas de Condorcet's account of Newton as an avatar of human progress. This line of inquiry is especially salient for examining the claims of authority that surround evolutionary depictions of human origins, given Charles Darwin's own mention of Newton as a scientific figure with whom he strongly identified. Writing in 1793, Condorcet described Newton's achievements in quasi-religious terms of revelation:

> Thus man at last discovered one of the physical laws of the universe, a law that has hitherto remained unique, like the glory of the man who revealed it. A hundred years of labor have confirmed the law which appears to govern all celestial phenomena to a degree that is, so to say, miraculous. Every time that a phenomenon appears not to come under that law, this uncertainty soon becomes the occasion of a new triumph.[17]

Even in this early text, the character of the scientist as revealer takes on almost as much significance as the revelation itself. Subsequently, the heroic figure of the scientist would be a prominent feature of public discourse about science.

Terrall continues by describing how the intellectual achievements of scientific data collection were buttressed by descriptions of the arduous physical labor involved in the scientist's work. At the same time, this account of physical prowess and endurance established the scientist as a figure of particular masculine virtue and vigor.[18] Condorcet was not unique in conflating the physical and intellectual rigors to be faced, and transcended, by early-modern scientists. Terrall also notes that the same themes appear, for example, in the writing of the eighteenth-century French mathematician Pierre Louis Maupertuis, and specifically in his description of "his laborious calculations in the frigid nights of the wilderness."[19]

17. M.-J.-A.-N. Caritat de Condorcet, quoted in Terrall, "Heroic Narratives of Quest and Discovery," 98.

18. Terrall, "Heroic Narratives of Quest and Discovery," 96.

19. Terrall, "Heroic Narratives of Quest and Discovery," 98.

This combination of physical daring and intellectual virtuosity set scientific exploration within the logic of discovery and conquest. As such, it fit neatly into the broader politic that characterized the modern European colonial project, where "stories of expeditions resonated with traditional notions of glory associated with military exploits," and "exploration of the abstract world of geometrical and algebraic relations paralleled a new kind of exploration of the physical world, where measurements and calculations were the objects of the quest."[20] While Terrall focuses on the narration of discoveries in the physical sciences and mathematics in the seventeenth and eighteenth centuries, the same image of the scientist would predominate in the nineteenth century, as biology emerged as the focus of both scholarly endeavor and popular attention.

Another helpful perspective may be found in Lorraine Daston and Peter Galison's description of scientific objectivity as the willed suppression of subjectivity. Daston and Galison suggest the notion of objectivity emerged in tandem with the development of industrial capitalism in the nineteenth century, as "a pulsing industrial economy and educational institutions based on competitive examination created 'new men,' who understood their rise to fame and fortune as a triumph of the will."[21] However, that era's understanding of human will and the human subject was itself a reaction to the "'vertiginous violence' of nineteenth century scientific progress."[22] The "opposition between objective science and subjective art" that characterized it was, in part, an attempt to maintain a sense of stability in the midst of accelerating change, where "scientists grasped at the new conceptual tools of subjectivity and objectivity in an attempt to reconcile progress and permanence."[23] These new conceptual tools would neither stay confined to the laboratory, nor be limited to the professional practitioners of science. Notions of objectivity and subjectivity, or popularized versions of them, would propagate throughout the modern Western nations where science— and scientists—claimed an increasingly authoritative cultural role.

One key to this claim of cultural authority lay in setting out the normative virtues that placed the scientist among the professional classes. This took place even as the physical as well as intellectual demands of the work were emphasized in the popular imagination. Where "the doctrine

20. Terrall, "Heroic Narratives of Quest and Discovery," 99.
21. Daston and Galison, *Objectivity*, 202.
22. Daston and Galison, *Objectivity*, 202.
23. Daston and Galison, *Objectivity*, 212.

of science as endless work, fueled by an unflagging will . . . echoed the platitudes of industrializing economies, and in some cases the analogy between labor in the laboratory and labor in the factory was made literal." At the same time, a contrast was drawn "between the humdrum, mechanical associations of work on the shop floor and the rather more elevated self-image of the man of science" deserving of "respect and remuneration at least comparable to the well-established liberal professions and, in certain instances, cultural authority equal to or greater than that enjoyed by either the clergy or men of letters."[24]

This authority was based not only on intellectual competence, but on a set of particular, and particularly masculine, virtues:

> A hero must do battle with a worthy foe, and it was themselves whom the heroes of objectivity met upon the field of honor. It was precisely because the man of science was portrayed as a man of action, rather than as a solitary contemplative, that the passive stance of the humble acolyte of nature, who (as Bernard put it) listens patiently to her answers to his questions without interrupting, required a mighty effort of self-restraint.[25]

Here, the (male) figure of the scientist is placed in the position of interrogating (female) nature. The form of subjectivity required for this work of manly action and mental self-control was thus portrayed as heroically virtuous.

Finally, Daston and Galison explain that the stereotypical figure of the scientist that emerged in the nineteenth century was just that—a stereotype—but nonetheless it worked on a normative level both in the scientific community and in the public imagination:

> A stereotype is a category of social perception, and a norm is no less a norm for being honored in the breach. Because epistemology is by definition normative—how knowledge should best be sought—there is no avoiding its do's and don'ts. Yet in the case of the lives of the learned, including scientists, bare treatises on method have never been deemed sufficient: the pursuit of knowledge is also a way of life, to be exemplified and thereby typified.[26]

---

24. Daston and Galison, *Objectivity,* 230.

25. Daston and Galison, *Objectivity,* 231.

26. Daston and Galison, *Objectivity,* 232.

How those lives are narrated, then, takes on normative as well as descriptive significance.

The work of these historians and theorists of science is indubitably helpful in locating, and critiquing, the figure of the scientific man within the Western history of ideas. At the same time, the limitations of many critical engagements with science become clear when applied to evolutionary biology. In this discipline in particular, race has loomed as an irreducible and unavoidable presence throughout its history, and many studies of science struggle to unpack the depth to which race plays a role within scientific logics. I suggest that any appraisal of evolutionary science and of scientific man as a cultural trope must also take race into account—not as an afterthought, but as a third dimension of critique.

The racial entanglements of evolutionary theory have been clear since its beginnings. Writing in the early nineteenth century, physician and printer William Charles Wells published a monograph that would contain the first use of the term "natural selection" in print. Wells's argument opens with the medical case history of Hannah Ward, a young English woman described in the title (and subsequently) as "a female of the white race, part of whose skin resembled that of a Negro."[27] His reflections on natural selection proceed from that basis, from which he eventually suggests that skin color variation is a result of racial resistance to disease. Returning to the case of Hannah Ward, Wells argues that if she were indeed becoming black in some sense, it would imply that racial difference cannot be a mark of a different species, but of variations within human beings as a whole. He claims that since a living being cannot change from one species to another, then blackness must represent a different morphology of the same species.

At the same time, he arranges the various races along a differential trajectory of development and civilization. For Wells, the divergence of Africans from European standards of beauty is a mark of their low state of civilization. Comparatively, he writes that the inhabitants of the Indian subcontinent have hair and features that more closely resemble those of a European, and that their physiognomy marks their closer cultural and civilizational proximity to the white ideal. Meanwhile, the blackness of Africans stands as a sign—or perhaps even a cause—of their degradation. They have, he argues, been slaves throughout history, and they are destined to always be so. In the writing of William Charles Wells, we see that from its beginnings, evolutionary logic has been tightly intertwined with a racial

27. Wells, *Account of a Female of the White Race*, 437.

imaginary and a trajectory of progress that places the white, Western man, who personifies reason and civilization, at its apex.

While some contemporary scholarship on the history and philosophy of science elides this racialized dimension, Denise Ferreira da Silva discusses it at length and provides a theoretical basis for understanding it in *Toward a Global Idea of Race*. Race, she writes, is "an effect of scientific signification" that also institutes what she calls *homo scientificus*, or scientific man. The emergence of scientific man as an archetypal figure and a theoretical category is, for Ferreira da Silva, a result of placing some humans into the register of the transcendental, through the "re-fashioning of self-consciousness" by the tools of universal reason.[28]

Ferreira da Silva's work is far too complex to grapple with in full in the course of this section, but her account of Darwinian, Western *homo scientificus*—as well as his Hegelian progenitor *homo historicus*—is crucial to a fuller understanding of the logic at work in historical and contemporary accounts of human origins based in an evolutionary narrative. *Toward a Global Idea of Race* is an attempt to answer the question of how whiteness came to "signify the transparent I," the self-narrating self who is completely aligned with reason, and "blackness to signify otherwise." Gender plays a role as well, so that what she describes as "the female racial subaltern" has "been consistently (re)produced" as one to whom "neither juridic universality nor self-determination applies."[29] Yet Ferreira da Silva's approach diverges from that of many contemporary scholars, locating the roots of racial subjection at a much deeper level than the intermittent racist statements of many key figures in modern Western thought. As she explains,

> Though I recognize the relevance of statements by Hobbes, Locke, Hume, Kant, and Hegel that explicitly place non-Europeans outside the trajectory of universal reason, I find the explicit exclusions they deploy insufficient to institute racial subjection. . . . My engagement with the founding statements of modern thought departs from postmodern critics' and racial theorists' approaches precisely because I am interested in the most subtle and yet powerful tools of racial subjection, the ones that the sociologic of exclusion (and its resilient metaphors "double consciousness," the "veil," and "the color line") can never capture precisely because of its privileging of historicity—that which nurses projects of a "post-racial" future where the expansion of universality would finally

28. Ferreira da Silva, *Toward a Global Idea of Race*, 113.
29. Ferreira da Silva, *Toward a Global Idea of Race*, 9.

include the others of Europe in the conception of being human that the transparency thesis produces. For racial subjection is as an effect of the desire that writes post-Enlightenment Europe in transparency and necessarily demands the obliteration of the others of Europe, historic strategies that cannot help the critical task.[30]

Scientific universality, then, does work that once was performed by theology, governing the modern production of Western man as a transparent "I." At the same time, Ferreira da Silva warns against any thought that racial subjection may in time be eliminated by including previously subjected people within that scientific universal. Racial subjection, for Ferreira da Silva, is generated by the creation of the transparent "I" itself.

Homo scientificus, Ferreira da Silva's term for the version of "man" that emerged in the nineteenth and early twentieth centuries, is a philosophical descendent of Hegel. But it differs from Hegel insofar as scientific universality makes transcendental *poesis,* the "rewriting of reason as a transcendental force," a matter of the body rather than of the spirit.[31] The difference between the Hegelian *homo historicus* and the later Darwinian *homo scientificus* is that the latter "assumes that in the body of man resides the causes for the emergence of the self-determined 'I,'"[32] Ferreira da Silva argues that this shift could only take place after scientific efforts to uncover the "truth of man" had sought to "rewrite the mind as an object of scientific reason."[33] As she explains, the scientific self that is transparent to reason is also the self whose "bodily and social configurations" signify its own transcendence.[34] The distinction between white, Western *homo scientificus* and other human beings, then, is not merely a matter of cultural difference that can be overcome by liberal rhetorics of inclusion. It is the chasm between the transcendental and the immanent, the mark of the creature who has placed himself in the position of the Creator.

The implications of this transcendental move become clear as Ferreira da Silva turns directly to the work of Darwin. The transparent *I* within which Darwin includes himself, Newton, Shakespeare, and the English colonial project, is set apart from the forces of nature as the victor. She writes,

---

30. Ferreira da Silva, *Toward a Global Idea of Race,* 14–15.
31. Ferreira da Silva, *Toward a Global Idea of Race,* xvi.
32. Ferreira da Silva, *Toward a Global Idea of Race,* 94.
33. Ferreira da Silva, *Toward a Global Idea of Race,* 94.
34. Ferreira da Silva, *Toward a Global Idea of Race,* 94.

When he explicitly writes the transparent I . . . outside—always already the winner—of the "struggle for Life," Darwin introduces an element absent in previous . . . descriptions of the global as a site of human differentiation, namely affectability. In the same statement, his version of the science of life safely places post-Enlightenment Europe in the moment of transparency and writes the "savage races" in the same way Newton has described the bodies of physics, as doubly governed by exteriority, that is, the exterior regulating force (productive nomos) and coexisting more powerful human beings, that is, the "Caucasian races." In other words, they are always already losers in the "struggle for existence" against the European "races of men," the ones whose social configurations testify to their competitive advantage.[35]

While the "savage races" are subject to both the laws of nature and the domination of other, more powerful, humans, the transparent *I* of post-Enlightenment Europe is subject to neither. For Darwin, European particularity necessarily entails sovereignty over both nature and other human beings, such that "Darwin's version of the science of life successfully rewrites living nature as a stage of the unfolding of transcendental poesis," the act by which the self is made transparent to reason and thus transcends creaturely existence. Ferreira da Silva explains that "always already a self-determined thing, in Darwin's version" the "'civilized man' remains (as a transparent thing) . . . beyond the means of 'natural selection.' He alone is self-producing; he alone enjoys the ability of self-perfection."[36] In other words, those who write science and scientific histories place themselves outside of the histories they narrate for others.

From this transcendental pinnacle, modern European man maps the unfolding of the world according to geography and time. This mapping process places the social structures of post-Enlightenment Europe at the pinnacle of development, a philosophical tactic that can be traced to Hegel's account of the unfolding of Spirit and the developmental trajectory of civilization.[37] Darwin would continue the process that Hegel began, making the particularities of Spirit a matter of particular bodies as well. This writing of European transcendentality, from a place at the apex of time yet also outside it, marks the depth to which evolutionary accounts of human origins cannot be made theologically harmless with a few cosmetic

35. Ferreira da Silva, *Toward a Global Idea of Race*, 94.
36. Ferreira da Silva, *Toward a Global Idea of Race*, 111.
37. Ferreira da Silva, *Toward a Global Idea of Race*, 86.

alterations. Their problems are rooted in their theoretical structure. Like the magi after encountering the newborn Jesus, we as Christians find we must go home "by another road" entirely.[38]

For Then the Whole Thing Would Collapse

One starting point along that other road lies in the work of Søren Kierkegaard. Reacting against the self-confident and bourgeois Lutheranism of his day, Kierkegaard began a theological trajectory that would continue with Karl Barth's commentary on Romans, whereby human overconfidence is replaced with a recursive self-questioning, and where the focus of the reader is repeatedly returned to the cross and the atoning work of Christ as the only possible starting point for theology. While Barth later differed with Kierkegaard on several points, notably on the contours and requirements of Christian love and the theological role of repetition, he maintained an affinity with Kierkegaard's thought that began with the writing of *The Epistle to the Romans* and continued to the end of his life. Upon being awarded the Sonning Prize in 1963, Barth used the occasion to address the role of Kierkegaard in his own thought, most explicitly in the *Römerbrief* period:

> [Kierkegaard] entered my thinking to a more serious and greater extent only in about 1919, at a critical juncture between the first and second editions of my *Epistle to the Romans*, and from that time onwards he played an important role in my writing. By 1916 a number of us of the younger generation had hesitantly set out to introduce a theology better than that of the nineteenth century and of the turn of the century—better in the sense that in it God, in his unique position over against man, and especially religious man, might clearly be given that honour we believed we found him to have in the Bible.[39]

For Barth, Kierkegaard's work was a necessary disruption of the "attempts to make the scriptural message innocuous" and the "excessively cheap Christianism and churchiness" that characterized much of nineteenth-century European Protestant theology.[40]

Kierkegaard is helpful not only as he helps us think differently about time and about the matter of beginnings, but also as he repeatedly punctures

38. Matt 2:12 (NRSV).
39. Barth, "Thank-You and a Bow," 97.
40. Barth, "Thank-You and a Bow," 99.

intellectual pretensions to authority—and the pose of respectability that comes through those pretensions. This section, as well as the sections on Kierkegaard that follow in the book, will include more extensive quotations from his texts. Because the whimsy and playfulness of his writing is an intrinsic part of his philosophical method, it may be helpful to the reader to experience the texts firsthand rather than at a distance. This immediacy, too, is part of his method.

In Kierkegaard's pseudonymous work *The Concept of Anxiety*, Vigilius Haufniensis ("The Watchman of Copenhagen") is the stereotypical example of one of his stock characters, the "assistant professor" who cites the trendiest academic authorities to enhance his own stature by association. As he explains in the preface, his reverence for a particular scholarly authority is based only on the dictates of intellectual fashion:

> When it comes to human authority, I am a fetish worshipper and will worship anyone with equal piety, but with one proviso, that it be made sufficiently clear by a beating of drums that he is the one I must worship and that it is he who is the authority and imprimatur for the current year. The decision is beyond my understanding, whether it takes place by lottery or balloting, or whether the honor is passed around so that each individual has his turn as an authority, like a representative of the burghers on the board of arbitration.[41]

Haufniensis's use of footnotes demonstrates his reliance on intellectual authority to ground himself. He cites several of Kierkegaard's other pseudonyms, including the manifestly unreliable Johannes de Silentio and Constantin Constantius, as well as the author(s) of *Either/Or*. The most notable example of this procedure is a footnote that extends across three pages, and that demonstrates Haufniensis's propensity to deploy the authority of others to confuse himself as well as his readers.[42]

We also find Kierkegaard playfully skewering the fashions of intellectual authority in the often-overlooked and fragmentary *Johannes Climacus*. This, the ostensible biography of the author of *Philosophical Fragments* and *Concluding Unscientific Postscript*, is especially helpful in uncovering the connections between those claims of authority, the attempt to construct an encyclopedic Hegelian system of knowledge, and anxiety around securing a proper beginning for thought. On one level, it revolves around three theses:

41. Kierkegaard, *Concept of Anxiety*, 8.
42. Kierkegaard, *Concept of Anxiety*, 17–19.

"(1) philosophy begins with doubt, (2) in order to philosophize, one must have doubted, and (3) modern philosophy begins with doubt."[43] But to read this text only as a meditation on doubt is, I believe, to miss much of the point. On another level, it functions as a caustic commentary on Hegelianism and the temporal relations contained in the Hegelian system's attempt to encompass all knowledge and thought.

The text begins with an easily missed parenthetical note. Under the heading, "Please Note," Kierkegaard writes,

> Someone who supposes that philosophy has never in all the world been so close as it is now to fulfilling its task of explaining all mysteries may certainly think it strange, affected, and scandalous that I choose the narrative form and do not in my small way hand up a stone to culminate the system. But someone who has become convinced that philosophy has never been so eccentric as now, never so confused despite all its definitions (much like the weather last winter when we heard simultaneously things never heard before at the same time—shouts of "mussels," "shrimp," and "watercress"—so that someone who was attentive to a particular shout at one moment would think it was winter, then spring, and then midsummer, while anyone who heard them all would think that nature had become confused and that the world would not last until Easter)—that person will surely find it in order that I, too, by means of the form seek to counteract the detestable untruth that characterizes recent philosophy, which differs from older philosophy by having discovered that it is ludicrous to do what a person himself said he would do or had done—he will find it in order and will merely lament, as I do, that the one who here begins this task has no more authority than I have.[44]

Here, we see Kierkegaard undermining his own authority, even as at the same time he contrasts his writing in the form of a whimsical narrative with the building up of the Hegelian system from its secure beginning in idealized thought.

That reliance on Hegelian philosophy is an underlying target of Kierkegaard's critique in Johannes Climacus. Climacus is described as a young man who is "ardently in love" with "thought, or more accurately, with thinking."[45] His particular love, of course, is for systematic thinking

---

43. Kierkegaard, *Johannes Climacus*, 132.

44. Kierkegaard, *Johannes Climacus*, 117.

45. Kierkegaard, *Johannes Climacus*, 118.

that is constructed from a beginning point, and thus he becomes obsessed with where to begin—so much so that he never finds the proper beginning he so desperately seeks. As Kierkegaard describes his predicament, "It was his delight to begin with a single thought and then, by way of coherent thinking, to climb step by step to a higher one, because to him coherent thinking was a *scala paradisi* [ladder of paradise], and his blessedness seemed to him even more glorious than the angels."[46] Yet Climacus is constantly frustrated by the precarity and instability of his own method. The system that he labored so carefully to build is constantly in danger of toppling. Temporarily coherent thought tends towards incoherence, and this is a property of human limitation:

> As long as he labored to climb up, as long as coherent thinking had as yet not managed to make its way, he was oppressed, because he feared losing all those coherent thoughts he had finished but which as yet were not perfectly clear and necessary. When we see someone carrying a number of fragile and brittle things stacked one upon the other, we are not surprised that he walks unsteadily and continually tries to maintain balance. If we do not see the stack, we smile, just as many smiled at Johannes Climacus, not suspecting that his soul was carrying a stack far taller than is usually enough to cause astonishment, that his soul was anxious lest one single coherent thought slip out, for then the whole thing would collapse. He did not notice that people smiled at him, no more than at other times he would notice an individual turn around in delight and look at him when he hurried down the street as lightly as in a dance. He did not pay any attention to people and did not imagine that they could pay any attention to him; he was and remained a stranger in the world.[47]

Perhaps we may smile, too, reading Kierkegaard's comic description of the difficulties entailed by piling one "coherent thought" upon another in the work of seamless system-building. It is the self-seriousness of this intellectual enterprise that itself invites parody—and, indeed, that can descend into a form of self-parody.

In the character of Johannes Climacus, we see a playful and poignant demonstration of a methodology of thought that depends on securing its own beginning and building the system from that point. It is a methodology that Kierkegaard identified in his many critiques of Hegel, of which

46. Kierkegaard, *Johannes Climacus*, 118.
47. Kierkegaard, *Johannes Climacus*, 119.

Johannes Climacus stands as one. It is also a methodology that Denise Ferreira da Silva identifies with the Hegelian and Darwinian figure of *homo modernus*, the world-historic and scientific man. Under this framework, the question of beginnings, of origins, becomes temporal as well as philosophical. The beginning of thought that defines humanity and human freedom is conflated with the temporal beginning of humanity. Evolutionary history is mapped onto anthropology.

Meanwhile, Johannes Climacus confuses himself with the question of the beginning and who has the authority to make it. Is it a "religious" or "historical" question, "ethical" or "metaphysical?"[48] He reflects that "to the Greeks," philosophy "begins with wonder," but concludes "a principle such as that can give rise to any historical consequence whatsoever."[49] Thinking further, he concludes that "modern philosophy" is "simultaneously the historical and the eternal" and "is aware of this itself." Indeed, he concludes "it is a union similar to the two natures in Christ."[50] He continues along this quasi-christological vein, tying his thoughts on modern philosophy and the question of where to make a philosophical beginning explicitly to the relationship of time and eternity:

> That the single individual could become conscious of the eternal, he could perhaps grasp, and an earlier philosophy presumably had thought to have grasped it, too—that is, if there had been any such thing at all. But to become conscious of the eternal in the whole historical concretion, indeed, according to the standard that it did not involve only the past, this he believed was reserved for the deity. Neither could he grasp at what instant in time a person would become so transfigured to himself that he, although himself present to himself, became past to himself. He believed that this had to be reserved for eternity and that eternity was only abstractly present in time.[51]

For Climacus, eternity is "only abstractly present" in time and so he takes recourse in an ecstatic meditation on the Hegelian unfolding of philosophy in a necessary chain:

> The individual philosopher must become conscious of himself and in this consciousness of himself also become conscious of his

48. Kierkegaard, *Johannes Climacus*, 153.
49. Kierkegaard, *Johannes Climacus*, 145.
50. Kierkegaard, *Johannes Climacus*, 139–40.
51. Kierkegaard, *Johannes Climacus*, 141.

significance as a moment in modern philosophy; in turn modern philosophy must become conscious of itself as an element in a prior philosophy, which in turn must become conscious of itself as an element in the historical unfolding of the eternal philosophy. Thus the philosopher's consciousness must encompass the most dizzying contrasts: his own personality, his little amendment—the philosophy of the whole world as the unfolding of the eternal philosophy.[52]

Kierkegaard's narration of the event continues with a wry depiction of the precariousness of a system that contains itself:

It was a long time before Johannes managed to think this enormous thought correctly and definitely. Just as a man rolling a heavy load up a mountain is often overcome so that his foot slips and the load rolls down, so it went with him. Finally he was confident that he could make the movement with ease. He then decided to let the thought work with all its weight, for he made a distinction between the laboriousness of thinking and the weight of the thought. As a historical thought, he thought the thought with ease. He had collected new strength, felt himself whole and complete; he put his shoulder, as it were, to the thought—and look, it overwhelmed him and he fainted![53]

The section "Modern Philosophy Begins with Doubt" ends with Climacus having made no progress towards understanding. It "cost him time and hard work," and he was "poorly rewarded for his troubles."[54] He concludes that his original thesis may have been "an impossibility," yet the sentence that follows is the most telling: "Yet he did not have the courage to believe this."[55]

In *Johannes Climacus*, we see the consequences of apprehending oneself as "a moment" in the necessary unfolding of the history of ideas. His recourse to systemic thought as the determinative "moment" in Climacus's own life evokes the "moment of transparency" in Ferriera da Silva's work in the previous section. In very different ways, both puncture the notion of the self-positing and self-narrating individual who achieves transcendence through reason. Both trouble the ways that an evolutionary or

52. Kierkegaard, *Johannes Climacus*, 140.

53. Kierkegaard, *Johannes Climacus*, 140–41.

54. Kierkegaard, *Johannes Climacus*, 143.

55. Kierkegaard, *Johannes Climacus*, 143.

developmental temporal consciousness, fixated on the question of its own origins, can obscure rather than reveal how humanity might think of itself in time.

But what if we begin elsewhere, not with the aim of securing a foundation for a Hegelian ladder of paradise, but from the nonabstract, revealed "moment" at the intersection of time and eternity? We see this moment further discussed in *Philosophical Fragments*, a text which, along with *Concluding Unscientific Postscript*, was published under the pseudonym of Johannes Climacus. In this, one of Kierkegaard's most abstract works, Climacus contrasts what he calls "the Socratic," a system in which truth lies within each individual and is achieved by an ascent of knowledge, with a version of Christian theology made newly strange. "If, then, the unity could not be brought about by an ascent, then it must be attempted by a descent."[56]

Climacus repeatedly returns to the phrase, "If the moment is to have decisive significance," gesturing towards a "moment" that determines human existence in something other than a remote temporal origin.[57] Over against the moment of transparency described by Ferreira da Silva, Kierkegaard focuses on the moment in which the human being receives herself by receiving the truth of her own sinfulness, and "discovers his untruth."[58] This is a knowledge that can neither be built up to by a Hegelian staircase or extracted from within the individual. Rather, it can only be received from the outside, and specifically from the Word made flesh, who took the form of a servant. And this, Climacus writes, is "the boundlessness of love, that in earnestness and truth and not in jest it wills to be the equal of the beloved, and it is the omnipotence of resolving love to be capable of that of which neither the king nor Socrates was capable."[59]

My reading of Kierkegaard concludes where it began, in *The Concept of Anxiety*. Continuing his initial honesty into the introduction, Haufniensis gives the reader several more clues for interpreting the anxiety-generating text on anxiety and sin that follows. "Whenever the issue of sin is dealt with," he writes, "one can observe by the very mood whether the concept is the correct one."[60] As he explains further:

56. Kierkegaard, *Philosophical Fragments*, 31.
57. Kierkegaard, *Philosophical Fragments*, 14.
58. Kierkegaard, *Philosophical Fragments*, 14.
59. Kierkegaard, *Philosophical Fragments*, 32.
60. Kierkegaard, *Philosophical Fragments*, 15.

> If sin is dealt with in metaphysics, the mood becomes that of dialectical uniformity and disinterestedness, which ponder sin as something that cannot withstand the scrutiny of thought. . . . If sin is dealt with in psychology, the mood becomes that of persistent observation, like the fearlessness of a secret agent, but not that of the victorious flight of earnestness out of sin. . . . Sin does not properly belong in any science, but it is the subject of the sermon, in which the single individual speaks to the single individual. In our day, scientific self-importance has tricked pastors into becoming something like professorial clerks who also serve science and find it beneath their dignity to preach.[61]

The "mood" of the "psychologically orienting" catalogue of observations that follows appears to be the wrong one. But Kierkegaard uses its "case histories" of anxiety and sin dialectically to create an anxious "holy hypochondria" in the reader.[62] By the end of this fun-house tour of anxiety and disorientation, the "single individual" reading the text is pushed away from detached observation, through a state of moral vertigo, and into an earnestness that "will rest only in the Atonement."[63] In the brief concluding section of the text, "Anxiety as Saving through Faith," the narrator finally turns from the 130-page pedagogy of anxiety to end in the pedagogy of Christ alluded to in 1 Thessalonians: "Concerning the love of the brethren you have no need to have anyone write to you, for you yourselves have been taught by God to love one another."[64] This is not a matter for abstract analysis, and it cannot be folded into a scholastic system. It is, instead, a matter of proclamation that awaits a response.

Yesterday, Today, and Forever

The grounding in the atonement that Kierkegaard repeatedly points toward in both *The Concept of Anxiety* and *Philosophical Fragments* is made even more explicit in the work of Karl Barth. In §47 of Volume III/2 of the *Church Dogmatics*, "Jesus, Lord of Time," Barth gives an account of creaturely temporality that separates itself conclusively from the anxiety about origins and scientific authority that appeared in previous sections.

---

61. Kierkegaard, *Concept of Anxiety*, 15–16.
62. Kierkegaard, *Concept of Anxiety*, 162.
63. Kierkegaard, *Concept of Anxiety*, 162.
64. 1 Thess 4:9 (NRSV).

For thinking differently about the question of origins, Barth's doctrine of creation is particularly helpful in three ways. First, he directs the reader beyond the unfruitful conversations about scientific modernity and Christian faith that define themselves in terms of conflicting or coherent worldviews. Second, he grounds his account of human life in time not on the development of the created world but on the unchanging person of Jesus Christ. Finally, he centers the time of humanity on what he calls the Easter history, making our own time dependent on the time of Jesus Christ crucified and raised from the dead.

By making the person and work of Jesus "at once the centre and the beginning and the end of all the lifetimes of all," Barth offers another way forward that avoids the usual debates over human origins that overwhelmingly, and unhelpfully, dominate many conversations around science and theology.[65] When confronted by efforts to tell a secular, scientific history that accounts for all that exists, Christians in the modern West have resorted to two polarities that are both produced by the same modernity to which they respond. It is easy enough for the proponents of dogmatic atheism to point to contemporary "creationists" as an object of ridicule. But it is far too easy for Christians to respond on the same terms, to try to merge evolutionism and a doctrine of creation into a seamlessly coherent worldview. Or, in the extreme case, they may attempt to do as Bultmann did, making modern, scientific reductionism determinative for doctrine and scriptural interpretation.

As Barth reminds his readers in this section, our situation is, and has always been, thankfully far more complicated and interesting than that. As he writes, "Is it our job as Christians to accept or reject world-views? Have not Christians always been eclectic in their world-views—and this for very good reasons?"[66] We are not forced into a false dichotomy between using "electric light and the wireless" and believing in "the New Testament world of demons and spirits."[67] As he puts it, the crux (quite literally) of the matter lies elsewhere:

> What if our radio-listeners recognized a duty of honesty which, for all this respect for the discoveries of modern science, is even more compelling than that of accepting without question the promptings of common sense? What if they felt themselves in a

65. Barth, *Church Dogmatics* III/2, 440.
66. Barth, *Church Dogmatics* III/2, 447.
67. Barth, *Church Dogmatics* III/2, 447.

position to give a free and glad and quite factual assent not to a
fides implicita in a world of spirits and demons but to faith in the
resurrection of Jesus Christ from the dead? What if they have no
alternative but to do this?[68]

Throughout this section of the doctrine of creation, Barth returns repeatedly to the idea that human existence in time is determined by the time of Easter, which is the time of cross and resurrection. In so doing, he ties this aspect of creation to the doctrine of reconciliation, replacing the question of origins with those of the atonement and the vindication of Jesus Christ in the resurrection. He also highlights one of the most curious features of dialogue between science and theology. The central Christian event is the person and work of Jesus Christ and his resurrection from the dead. Christian confession stands or falls on the claim that Jesus Christ is the incarnate Second Person of the Trinity. Yet science and theology have studiously avoided dialogue around this claim, focusing instead on the origins of the material world and of humanity.

For Barth, the event of cross and resurrection does not function as a new originary point in an unchanging and unchanged temporal sequence. Responding in particular to Oscar Cullmann's *Christ and Time*, Barth takes issue with the idea that "the New Testament authors started with a particular conception of time as an ascending series of aeons, and then inserted into this geometrical figure the event of Christ as the center of this line."[69] The constant factor is not time, but God. Jesus Christ, who is the same yesterday, today, and forever, irrupted into time and irreversibly changed it in doing so.

The constancy of Jesus is only possible in and through the time of Easter, the time of the resurrection, insofar as it erases the limitations of creaturely time. The time of the resurrection, the time of Jesus Christ, is "the time of the covenant; the great Sabbath; the year of salvation; fulfilled time." The barrier that time presents to other creatures is, for and in Christ, a gateway. The time of Jesus Christ is "not only the time of man, but the time of God, eternal time." As such, Christ "not only is in time and has time like other men, but He also is Lord of time."[70]

68. Barth, *Church Dogmatics* III/2, 447.

69. Barth, *Church Dogmatics* III/2, 443.

70. Barth, *Church Dogmatics* III/2, 464.

This argument does not place Jesus as a divine event within a pre-conceived philosophy of time. Instead, as Barth admits, it hinges on the confession that Jesus Christ is raised from the dead:

> If Christ were not risen from the dead, our treatment of the whole subject would have no basis whatever in the Word and revelation of God. Every assertion beyond the mere fact that Jesus' time was like all other times in that it had beginning, duration, and end, would be mere speculation, a house of cards built on our subjective impression of his life in time, and liable to collapse at the slightest touch of justifiable doubts as to the validity of our subjective impression and therefore our competence. Jesus is the Lord of time in the sense expounded because He is the Son of God, and as such the eternal God in person, the Creator of all time and thus its sovereign Ruler.[71]

Barth's project—as well as this project—depends at the deepest level on the confession of the Triune God and of the resurrection of Jesus Christ.

While *Church Dogmatics* III/2 is part of the doctrine of creation, Barth's consideration of human existence in time proceeds not from the moment of creation but from the time of God through and in Jesus Christ. The exegetical hinge of §47 is Hebrews 13:8, "Jesus Christ is the same yesterday, today, and forever." As Barth explains, both this verse and his theological reflection on creaturely existence in time hinge on cross and resurrection:

> Jesus Christ belongs not only to yesterday, or to-day, or an indefinite future. He belongs to all times simultaneously. He is the same Christ in all of them. There is no time which does not belong to him. He really is the Lord of time. If we ask the author of Hebrews how he came to attribute to Jesus this extraordinary being in time, the only answer which he can give is to refer to the point indicated a few verses later (Hebrews 13:20). Who is 'our Lord Jesus'? He is the great Shepherd of the sheep in the blood of the covenant, whom the God of peace 'brought again from the dead.' He is the great High Priest who 'hath passed through the heavens' (4:14) to sit down at the right hand of the Majesty on high, i.e. God. (1:3; 8:1; 10:12; 12:2). Unless we are prepared to understand 13:8 in the light of these other passages, and therefore of the Easter axiom of the New Testament author too, we shall not understand it at all.[72]

---

71. Barth, *Church Dogmatics* III/2, 464–65.
72. Barth, *Church Dogmatics* III/2, 466.

At the beginning the next section (§48, "Given Time"), Barth explains that a theological consideration of our time as human beings can only proceed from this basis. Because Jesus Christ is the Lord of time, and because his time through the work of cross and resurrection is fulfilled time, the time of Christ encompasses creaturely time as the risen Lord takes our time to himself. As this fullness of time in Jesus Christ embraces our time, it gives our time back to us again, no longer as a possession to be grasped or as a matter of fear, but as a liberating gift.

In the next subsection of §47, Barth expands on this notion of time as gift. While discussions of time as gift are almost ubiquitous in theological discourse, Barth is distinguished by making this gift completely determined in and by Christ, rather than in or by the creative act of God in itself. As he writes, "the existence of the man Jesus in time is our guarantee that time as the form of human existence is in any case willed and created by God, is given by God to man, and is therefore real."[73] Human existence in time is, for Barth, a continuous positive act of divine preservation:

> Surprising as it is, it is to the free grace of God in Jesus Christ that we owe the fact that the nature in which we were created, and from which we have fallen by falling away from God, is not taken away from us, but is maintained and preserved; that in spite of the falsehood in which we have become involved we may be genuinely in time and have true and genuine time.[74]

Continuing in an excursus, Barth emphasizes the importance of grounding reflection on time in Jesus Christ and not in any form of natural theology. He writes,

> To see the truth of this, we have only to cease trying to ignore the free grace of God in Jesus Christ. We have only to cease trying to make use of "natural" theology and therefore anthropology. Illusion always results when we seek light on human nature from any other source than the man Jesus Christ. To do so is to trifle with the fact of sin. It is to dig leaking wells. It is to entangle ourselves in conjectures and reinterpretations. It is again to seek final refuge in oblivion. The profound unrest concerning our corrupted nature and our forfeiture of time remains unassuaged. The only real way to meet it is the way which the righteous God, who is merciful in His righteousness, has taken, takes and will take to all eternity in

---

73. Barth, *Church Dogmatics* III/2, 520.
74. Barth, *Church Dogmatics* III/2, 520.

Jesus Christ. The only genuinely victorious protest against it is His protest against our contradiction, which is also His protest against its consequences and therefore against our perishing, against the possibility that His creature will cease to be His creature. This divine protest is the rock on which we take our stand when we count on it that there is a human nature preserved for man in spite of his fall, and therefore a true and genuine being of man in time. There is no other ground on which we can seriously make this claim. But on this ground the claim can and must be made seriously.[75]

Determined by and in Christ, the time which is given to human beings takes on a new and different significance as the form of human existence.[76] To be human is to be in time, but to be a human being in Christ is to live in time but not as a captive to time. As the Lord of time, Jesus "stands at the beginning of all our attempted thinking about time, ruling and establishing, illuminating and proving."[77] At this beginning stands the end of all "false and cheerless conceptions of time."[78]

Where can a theological reflection on time begin? Where does the story of who we are as human beings begin? For Barth, there is only one answer to both questions: the cross and resurrection of Jesus Christ. As he writes, "if we make this our starting point, we shall find it possible and necessary, compelling and illuminating, to break through and invert the concept of time along the lines attempted. Yet we shall not forget that this starting point is not a formula to be adopted and appropriated at will, but an actual encounter with the reality to which theological presentation can only point."[79] It is to the matter of this "actual encounter" that this chapter finally turns.

One purpose of this work is to draw a repeated and distinct contrast between an account of time circumscribed by scientific modernity and another vision of time that is at once christological and liturgical. Theologically speaking, this version of liturgical time begins at the fixed point whereby the story of Jesus Christ becomes our story: in the cross and resurrection, in the events through which Christ is Lord of time. Liturgically, this is at once the time of Good Friday and Easter and also the time of baptism. This time of dying and being raised again to new life in Christ is reflected in

75. Barth, *Church Dogmatics* III/2, 520.
76. Barth, *Church Dogmatics* III/2, 552.
77. Barth, *Church Dogmatics* III/2, 552.
78. Barth, *Church Dogmatics* III/2, 552.
79. Barth, *Church Dogmatics* III/2, 553.

the prayer over the water in the baptismal liturgy, as it recalls that through the waters of baptism "we are buried with Christ in his death" and "share in his resurrection."[80] Over and against all questions of origins that seek to locate human meaning in biology, or in a just-so story composed through speculation on an evolutionary past that inevitably becomes a tale of political destiny, the events of cross and resurrection offer an alternative place from which to begin.

It is in cross and resurrection that our time is determined and given back to us again. And our participation in cross and resurrection in Christ, through the sacraments of baptism and Eucharist, is the starting place for any consideration of time to follow. This is the place from which we begin, and begin again, in theological reflection that is rooted in—and in service to—the work of proclamation. As Barth writes in *Church Dogmatics* I/2,

> It is from the standpoint of baptism and the Lord's Supper that the prophets and apostles, and in their turn the fathers and Reformers, are really fixed: and fixed in such a way that we cannot evade them. And it is when regarded in the light of baptism and the Lord's Supper that, parallel to every temporal movement in time in which it must occur, preaching too must and will always acquire that particular element of fixity, of unchanging similarity to itself, without which it ceases in any really effective way to bear witness by the mouth of man. *Et incarnatus est.*[81]

United with Christ in the paschal mystery through baptism, the Christian life in time is characterized both by an aspect of the once-for-all nature of the resurrection and the repetition of the Eucharist that is always yet to come, even as we anticipate the eschatological banquet at the end of time. This is, for Barth, where theology does its work:

> The sphere of sacrament means the sphere in which man has to think of himself as on the way from the baptism already poured out upon him to the Lord's Supper yet to be dispensed to him, the sphere in which he begins with faith in order to reach faith. On this way our perception will certainly be a true one if we think of ourselves as the recipients of revelation. And it is in this sphere that theology has to seek both its beginning and its goal, and by the law of this sphere that it must direct its methods.[82]

---

80. *Book of Common Prayer 1979*, 306–7.
81. Barth, *Church Dogmatics* I/2, 231.
82. Barth, *Church Dogmatics* I/2, 232.

Rather than contend with, be mystified by, or accommodate itself to, various narratives of origins grounded in scientific authority, theology is called to begin elsewhere. It is perhaps no coincidence that contemporary American debates centered on science and Christian faith tend to cluster around questions of creation rather than redemption. While creation can be argued about from a standpoint of detachment, the crucified and risen Christ encounters us and demands a response.

3

Endings

Once when the price of spices in Holland fell, the merchants had a few
cargoes sunk in the sea in order to jack up the price. This was an excusable,
perhaps even necessary, deception. Do we need something similar in the
world of the spirit? Are we so sure that we have achieved the highest, so
that there is nothing left for us to do except piously to delude ourselves into
thinking that we have not come that far, simply in order to have something
to occupy our time? . . . Whatever one generation learns from another,
no generation learns the essentially human from a previous one. In this
respect, each generation begins primitively, has no task other than what each
previous generation had, nor does it advance further, insofar as the previous
generations did not betray the task and deceive themselves.

—SØREN KIERKEGAARD, *FEAR AND TREMBLING*[1]

"I am the Alpha and the Omega," says the Lord God,
"who is and who was and who is to come, the Almighty."

—REVELATION 1:8 (NRSV)

"Winter is coming."
Maybe it should come as no surprise that this line from
the popular fantasy novel and television series *Game of Thrones* became a

1. Kierkegaard, *Fear and Trembling*, 121.

catchphrase in post-recession America. In an era of war abroad and auster-
ity at home, when the lines between the foreign and the domestic have been
unveiled as the mirages that they are, perhaps a fictional world based on
tight-knit clans living through bad days and preparing for worse to come
was bound to resonate with viewers. But the televised version of *Game of
Thrones* has not been the only recent appearance of this phrase. It also plays
a key role in *The Fourth Turning*, a work of popularized social and political
science that reportedly influences the nationalist political project of former
White House advisor Stephen Bannon.[2] In the opening chapter of the text,
entitled "Winter Comes Again," Strauss and Howe write, "America feels like
it's unraveling. Though we live in an era of relative peace and comfort, we
have settled into a mood of pessimism about the long-term future, fear-
ful that our superpower nation is somehow rotting from within."[3] National
decay calls for national rebirth.

Strauss and Howe's argument proceeds from that point, building on
the idea that the life of the nation is based on a cyclical pattern of generational shifts. As they explain,

1. The First Turning is a High, an upbeat era of strengthening institutions and weakening individualism, when a new civic order
   implants and the old values regime decays.
2. The Second Turning is an Awakening, a passionate era of spiritual upheaval, when the civic order comes under attack from a
   new values regime.
3. The Third Turning is an Unraveling, a downcast era of strengthening individualism and weakening institutions, when the old
   civic order decays and the new values regime implants.
4. The Fourth Turning is a Crisis, a decisive era of secular upheaval,
   when the values regime propels the replacement of the old civic
   order with a new one.[4]

Writing in 1997, they contended that America at the turn of the millennium was due for a national crisis and that the nation needed to prepare
accordingly. As they explain, "History is seasonal, and winter is coming.

2. In the wake of the 2016 election, it has become a cottage industry among certain
sectors of the press to divine the philosophical underpinnings of Trumpism, Bannonism,
and the various strands of the "alt-right" movement. See, for example, Peters, "Bannon's
Worldview"; Johnson and Stokols, "What Steve Bannon Wants You to Read"; or Howe,
"Where Did Steve Bannon Get His Worldview?"

3. Strauss and Howe, *Fourth Turning*, 1.

4. Strauss and Howe, *Fourth Turning*, 3.

Like nature's winter, the secular winter can come early or late. A Fourth Turning can be long and difficult, brief but severe, or (perhaps) mild. But, like winter, it cannot be averted. It must come in its turn."[5] In more recent years, they have suggested the 2008 financial crisis marked the beginning of the predicted societal cataclysm. This pattern of strength, decline, and rebirth through struggle, we are told, is the proper way to read the past in order to shape a new and resurgent American future.

In the previous chapter, I focused on the question of beginnings and the problem of origins. I turn now to the future, and ultimately to questions of eschatology. These two problems are intimately related, as narratives of origins are habitually used to legitimate a particular vision of destiny, or to shape the future in accordance with a predetermined agenda. Yet, the origin defined by cross and resurrection described in the first chapter is also inextricably linked to Christian expectation and Christian hope. The connection between the past and future that is received in and through Christ lies at the heart of many eucharistic prayers, including the Orthodox Liturgy of St. James and the current Roman Missal, as well as Anglican and Lutheran liturgies: "Christ has died, Christ is risen, Christ will come again."[6]

At the same time, contemporary American political discourse seems to be defined, or perhaps captured, by two contesting visions of the national and global future. The first is a globalized, technocratic model in which science plays the role previously reserved to revelation. This vision of the future deploys an immanentist eschatology that encompasses both technological progress and moral development, and points towards the culmination of a continuously unfolding global process. Moreover, theological versions of this progressive future can be seen in works from the nineteenth century to the present, from Victorian Anglican Charles Kingsley to Social Gospel pioneer Walter Rauschenbusch to Jesuit Pierre Teilhard de Chardin and contemporary attempts to recover his work.

The second vision of the future is a reaction to progressivism and globalization. It may take the form of a resurgent nationalism and an appeal for the reestablishment of Christendom—albeit a Christendom without Christ. While this version of the future rejects narratives of progress, it does so by means of a cyclical vision of time, where periodic conflagrations function as necessary stages in world history. This is not a linear,

---

5. Strauss and Howe, *Fourth Turning*, 6.

6. *Book of Common Prayer 1979*, 363.

progressive unfolding of history, but it combines the notions of repetition on a historical scale with a teleology of national destiny and unity. The vision of national crisis and national unity espoused by Strauss, Howe, and Bannon falls into this category. Another response to globalized progressivism is found in the philosophies of authoritarianism and hyper-capitalism espoused by the "neo-reaction" and "Dark Enlightenment" movements I will describe in this chapter.

What these seemingly disparate accounts share is perhaps more important than their differences. They are shaped and produced by scientific modernity and the reactions to it. They depend on an account of necessary sacrifice, where the lives of some human beings are seen as the unavoidable and often necessary collateral damage of the process of securing the future of the social body. To examine these similarities and differences further, I turn first to the progressive vision of the future as it emerged in the nineteenth century and flourished in the following decades.

Theologies of the Future

A Universal Law of Living Things: Charles Kingsley

In the name of generating a seamless and systematic account that includes both the Christian tradition and natural selection, what has too often resulted has been a theology of success, written from the position of transparency by those who are always, already the winners in an evolutionary struggle. It has been the case since the early days of Darwinism, when the Rev. Canon Charles Kingsley delivered a lecture entitled "The Natural Theology of the Future" at Sion College in London. For Kingsley, the imperative of progress required that Anglican theology adapt itself to the latest developments of scientific thought in order to appeal to a scientifically informed, modern nation.

Kingsley regards the preaching of John Wesley and George Whitfield as incompatible with this theological future, writing that "there lingers about them a savor of the old monastic theory, that this earth is the devil's planet, fallen, accursed, goblin haunted, needing to be exorcised at every turn before it is useful or even safe for man."[7] However, the planet was governed by scientific laws that ensured it would be safer for some than for others. In one passage, he writes:

7. Kingsley, "Natural Theology of the Future," 316.

Physical science is proving more and more the immense importance of Race; the importance of hereditary powers, hereditary organs, hereditary habits, in all organized beings . . . She is proving more and more the omnipresent action of the differences between races, how the more favored race (she cannot avoid using the epithet) exterminates the less favored, or at least expels it . . . and, in a word, that competition between every race and every individual of that race, and reward according to deserts is (as far as we can see) a universal law of living things.[8]

Under this logic, the depredations of colonialism are naturalized by those who see themselves as the transcendent success stories of evolutionary development. Evolution's failures, in this scenario, are getting exactly what they deserve, while the future belongs to the winners of Darwinian struggle.

An International and Purely Human Religion: Walter Rauschenbusch

Another, slightly later, attempt to secure the future through the convergence of theology, evolutionary theory, and politics can be seen in the work of the Social Gospel pioneer Walter Rauschenbusch. In April 1907, he published *Christianity and the Social Crisis*, the work that would, in the words of one biographer, "catapult [him] into national prominence."[9] Throughout this seminal text, Rauschenbusch defines his project of social and religious progress over against an apocalyptic vision of Christianity. The notion of a divinely instituted discontinuity in history was, for Rauschenbusch, an artifact of the Jewish experience of loss of national power, and not to be interpreted as normative.[10] In fact, the apocalyptic impulse in Christianity is a problem to be interpreted away, or to be set aside as a less-well-developed stage in the emergence of an ideal form of Christianity. It is an error in which "the Church spilled a little of the lurid colors of its own apocalypticism over the loftier conceptions of its Master."[11] In Rauschenbusch's thought, the apocalyptic aspects of Christianity were consigned to an intermediate historical stage. In doing so, he separated them from the

8. Kingsley, "Natural Theology of the Future," 324.

9. Minus, *Walter Rauschenbusch*, 157.

10. Rauschenbusch, *Christianity and the Social Crisis*, 27.

11. Rauschenbusch, *Christianity and the Social Crisis*, 62–63.

ostensibly pure religion of which Jesus was the culmination of a continuous developmental trajectory.

For Rauschenbusch, Jesus was identified with an evolutionary, rather than revolutionary, approach to history, and to the role of Christianity within that history. He writes, "we do find in early Christianity a different type of thought which had the same high sense of an historical mission, but which combined it with a saner and more philosophical outlook on the world. It was evolutionary, while apocalypticism was catastrophic."[12] As the culminating evolutionary stage in the history of religion, Christianity would be uniquely poised to produce a new internationalism that was consonant with the optimism of the Progressive era.

This evolutionary emergence of Christianity was also associated with the evolution of social institutions, and in particular with the emergence of the Roman Empire as the prototype of the modern state. In an extended passage that bears quoting in full, he writes,

> When Christianity came on the stage of history, there were two distinct types in possession, the Gentiles and the Jews, with a deep and permanent cleavage between the two. Christianity added a third genus, and Christians were profoundly convinced that they were to assimilate and transform all others into a higher unity. The Epistle to the Ephesians is a tract reflecting on this aspect of the mission of Christ. Romans 9–11 is a philosophy of history, forecasting the method by which this process of absorption and solidification was to come about. There is a prophetic grandeur of vision in this large international outlook of the early Christians. The evolution of religion has always been intimately connected with the evolution of social organization. When tribes were amalgamated into a nation, tribal religions passed into a national religion. In the Roman Empire nations were now being fused into a still larger social unity. The old national religions were incapable of serving as the spiritual support for this vaster social body. There was a crying need for an international and purely human religion. Christianity, as we now know, was destined to fulfil this function, and these early Christian thinkers had a prophetic premonition of this destiny. They often dwelt on the fact that Christianity had been born simultaneously with the Empire under Augustus. The universal State and the universal religion were twins by birth. They ought, therefore, to be in helpful relations to each other in accordance with the manifest purpose of God. The Empire should cease

12. Rauschenbusch, *Christianity and the Social Crisis*, 63.

to persecute the Church. The Church could be the best ally of the State in creating civil peace, because Christians had the highest morality, and because they alone had power over the demons who menaced the security of the Empire. As the soul holds the body together, so Christians hold the world together. They exert a conservative and unifying influence. This conception of Christianity as a penetrating, renewing, and unifying power, destined to control the future of the world, was just as full of triumphant hopefulness as the apocalyptic hope, but allowed of a quiet process of historic growth. It did not regard the existing State as Satanic and evil, yet had full room for moral criticism of existing conditions and the determination to contribute to a thorough moral change. The apocalyptic hope was probably the dominant Christian conception of history in the very first generations. This other view gained power as time passed, as the number and influence of Christians increased, and as men of larger mental reach and higher education grew up in the Church.[13]

There are several points worth noting in this passage. The first is that Rauschenbusch clearly allies himself with the "men of larger mental reach and higher education" who espoused the latter, evolutionary view of history. The second is the precise nature of the relationship between the church and state that he recommends. The church is intended to be a reformist institution, recommending gradual changes in the direction of moral uplift, but not standing in opposition or resistance to the power of the state. Third, Rauschenbusch presents Christianity as a universal and universalizing force, capable of uniting human beings into a "higher unity." Finally, the parallels between the international scope of imperial Rome and early twentieth-century internationalism are also of interest. Later in the same section, Rauschenbusch makes these parallels explicit, noting the similarity between the Roman Empire centered on the Mediterranean and an emerging Transatlantic consensus.

In a subsequent chapter, Rauschenbusch combines this gradual developmental trajectory with a second facet of his argument. The present day, he contends, offers both an unprecedented crisis in Western social life and an unprecedented opportunity and capacity to respond effectively to that crisis. He finds hope in a reformist and gradualist program of moral and social uplift:

---

13. Rauschenbusch, *Christianity and the Social Crisis*, 114–15.

Without such a conception of the evolution of social institutions any larger idea of social regeneration could hardly enter the minds of men. The modern socialist movement is really the first intelligent, concerted, and continuous effort to reshape society in accordance with the laws of social development. The comprehension of the gradualness of social changes is also a late attainment. The childish mind wants swift results and loses interest if things move slowly. It wants the flower seeds which were planted last night to be above ground before breakfast. It finds the atmosphere of the fairy tales so congenial, because there great things happen at the waving of the fairy's wand. This is also the characteristic of the savage, and in lessening degree of every unscientific mind. It understands personal action, and so far as its personal powers will reach, it is willing to help in making things better. For anything beyond its immediate reach and power it trusts in divine intervention. For the slow moulding of institutions by ideas and the slow creation of ideas to justify institutions, for the steady alternation of cause and effect in the development of society, there has been no trained observation.[14]

Throughout this section, Rauschenbusch draws multiple analogies and connections between nineteenth- and twentieth-century advances in the natural and the social sciences. As Janet Fishburn notes, while he was opposed to individualistic notions of the "survival of the fittest," he did not hesitate to incorporate other aspects of social Darwinism into his thought. He may have replaced "the biological basis of Social Darwinism" with "an anthropological analogy of individuals and institutions," but the evolutionary logic remained the same.[15]

Paradoxically, this modern, scientific approach was also presented as a return to the ideals of Jesus himself, without what Rauschenbusch saw as the accretions of Hellenism and superstition. Jesus, he writes, "stood almost alone in the comprehension of the gradualness of moral conquest," which the fathers of the early church polluted with the "air of the miraculous" that was "directly hostile to any scientific comprehension of social facts" and the "real causes of things."[16]

Newly equipped with scientifically informed knowledge of "the real causes of things," Christianity would be uniquely poised to take its rightful place in the regeneration of the social order. As Rauschenbusch writes, "for

14. Rauschenbusch, *Christianity and the Social Crisis*, 116.

15. Fishburn, *Fatherhood of God and the Victorian Family*, 126.

16. Rauschenbusch, *Christianity and the Social Crisis*, 196.

the first time in religious history we have the possibility of so directing religious energy by scientific knowledge that a comprehensive and continuous reconstruction of social life in the name of God is within the bounds of human possibility."[17]

Christianity and the Social Crisis represented a stirring call to action aimed at those with the social and intellectual capital to turn the vision of the Social Gospel into a reality, the "statesmen, prophets, and apostles," the "strong" who "direct their love of power to the uplifting of the people" such that "the atrophied members of the social body will be filled with a fresh flow of blood; and a regenerate nation will look with the eyes of youth across the fields of the future."[18] The alternative to an embrace of this program is presented in stark, revealing terms. The turn of the twentieth century, Rauschenbusch contends, represents a unique convergence in the trajectory of history. Without decisive action, he argues, the fate of the West—and of Christendom—is in doubt:

> The cry of "Crisis! crisis!" has become a weariness. Every age and every year are critical and fraught with destiny. Yet in the widest survey of history Western civilization is now at a decisive point in its development. Will some Gibbon of Mongol race sit by the shore of the Pacific in the year A.D. 3000 and write on the "Decline and Fall of the Christian Empire"? If so, he will probably describe the nineteenth and twentieth centuries as the golden age when outwardly life flourished as never before, but when that decay, which resulted in the gradual collapse of the twenty-first and twenty-second centuries, was already far advanced. Or will the twentieth century mark for the future historian the real adolescence of humanity, the great emancipation from barbarism and from the paralysis of injustice, and the beginning of a progress in the intellectual, social, and moral life of mankind to which all past history has no parallel? It will depend almost wholly on the moral forces which the Christian nations can bring to the fighting line against wrong, and the fighting energy of those moral forces will again depend on the degree to which they are inspired by religious faith and enthusiasm. It is either a revival of social religion or the deluge.[19]

---

17. Rauschenbusch, *Christianity and the Social Crisis*, 285.

18. Rauschenbusch, *Christianity and the Social Crisis*, 285.

19. Rauschenbusch, *Christianity and the Social Crisis*, 285–86.

For Rauschenbusch, the survival of the West depends on the efforts of Christian men of action, whom he calls to seize the wheel of history and steer it in the direction of the civilized kingdom of God.

In a contemporary era that recalls the first Gilded Age in which Rauschenbusch was writing, the temptation is strong to recover the reformist energy of the Social Gospel for the present day. Yet, this is an ultimately false path towards incorporating concern for economic realities into Christian witness. The emphasis on evolutionary incrementalism, as well as the focus on an eschatology achieved by means of human effort, limit the promise of the Social Gospel's theology. Moreover, the Social Gospel movement, as espoused by Rauschenbusch and others, was concerned above all with maintaining societal order against the specters of sexual chaos and political anarchism that loomed in a newly urbanized America.

Writing as he did in the wake of the assassination of President William McKinley in 1901, Rauschenbusch appealed frequently to the perceived threat to the American social order posed by anarchism—a threat which was also closely associated with new immigrants to the United States from southern and eastern Europe.[20] Rauschenbusch's fear of revolutionary movements becomes explicit in the second half of *Christianity and the Social Crisis*. As he moves from universal statements about the essence of Christianity to concrete prescriptions, he posits a mediating role for the church—and for church leaders. Pastors were to act as go-betweens, advocating for the poor amongst the wealthy, while also keeping potentially explosive working-class anger in check:

20. *Christianity and the Social Crisis* was first published in 1907, four years after Congress passed the Immigration Act of 1903, which barred immigrants on the basis of their political beliefs for the first time since the Alien and Sedition Acts of 1798. The following categories were barred from entering the United States: "All idiots, insane persons, epileptics, and persons who have been insane within five years previous; persons who have had two or more attacks of insanity at any time previously; paupers; persons likely to become a public charge; professional beggars; persons afflicted with a loathsome or with a dangerous contagious disease; persons who have been convicted of a felony or other crime or misdemeanor involving moral turpitude; polygamists, anarchists, or persons who believe in or advocate the overthrow by force or violence of the Government of the United States or of all government or of all forms of law, or the assassination of public officials; prostitutes, and persons who procure or attempt to bring in prostitutes or women for the purpose of prostitution." Immigration Act of March 3, 1903, (32 Stat. 1213, ch.1012), https://www.loc.gov/law/help/statutes-at-large/57th-congress/session-2/c57s2ch1012.pdf.

A minister mingling with both classes can act as an interpreter to both. He can soften the increasing class hatred of the working class. He can infuse the spirit of moral enthusiasm into the economic struggle of the dispossessed and lift it to something more than a "stomach question." On the other hand, among the well-to-do, he can strengthen the consciousness that the working people have a real grievance and so increase the disposition to make concessions in practical cases and check the inclination to resort to force for the suppression of discontent. If the ministry would awaken among the wealthy a sense of social compunction and moral uneasiness, that alone might save our nation from a revolutionary explosion. It would be of the utmost importance to us all if the inevitable readjustment could be secured by a continuous succession of sensible demands on the one side and willing concessions on the other.[21]

The gradual evolutionary trajectory Rauschenbusch associates with true Christianity is deployed to maintain the social order in the midst of the depredations of the Gilded Age. The church, and those who serve it, are drafted into the service of that end—of keeping the lid on the pressure cooker of social tension.

Upward by Way of Forward: Pierre Teilhard de Chardin

Several patterns of thought that predominate in the thought of Kingsley and Rauschenbusch continue, and are in some ways intensified, in the writing of Pierre Teilhard de Chardin. Teilhard made a brief appearance in the previous chapter, and I turn now to his writing in more detail. For this Jesuit paleontologist, the convergence of evolutionary thought and theology took on paramount importance. Teilhard created a vision of the future in which the progress of creation would eventually be brought to its fulfillment through a continuous developmental trajectory of becoming.

For Teilhard, progress is no less than an article of faith. As he writes in *The Future of Man*, "Progress has not caused the action of Man (Man himself) to change in each separate individual; but because of it the action of human nature (Mankind) has acquired, in every thinking man, a fullness that is wholly new."[22] He continues by explaining that "Progress is a force, and the most dangerous of forces. It is the Consciousness of all that is and

21. Rauschenbusch, *Christianity and the Social Crisis*, 368.
22. Teilhard de Chardin, *Future of Man*, 18.

all that can be."[23] And, as such, it is a force through which human beings bring about the future collectively, in a "definitive act" in which "the total force of collective evolution will be released and flourish."[24] Teilhard shares with Rauschenbusch not only a faith in the outworking of progress, but also an emphasis on its continuity. Crucially, this continuity extends not only to the development of humanity but also to the person of Christ himself:

> From the commencement of things an Advent of ploughing and harvesting began, in the course of which, gently and lovingly, the determinisms reached out and moved towards the growing of a Fruit that was beyond hope and yet awaited. . . . And since the time when Jesus was born, when He finished growing and died and rose again, everything has continued to move because Christ has not yet completed His own forming. He has not yet gathered in to Himself the last folds of the Garment of flesh and love which His disciples are making for him. The mystical Christ has not yet attained His full growth. In the pursuance of this engendering is situated the ultimate spring of all created activity . . . Christ is the Fulfilment even of the natural evolution of beings.[25]

Here, the person of Christ is subject to the determination of ongoing evolutionary processes, and furthermore making that christological development dependent on the works of created beings.

Teilhard shares another feature with Rauschenbusch: a sense that the West is in a state of moral, political, and religious crisis whose only answer is a progressive movement—one that is neither revolutionary nor based on "the traditional upward impulse of religious worship."[26] It is not oriented around the radical transcendence of a God who is the Creator. Instead, he proposes a combination of "the Upward and the Forward," tracing a continuous, linear path towards a divine and human (or "ultra-human") future. This trajectory represents an eschatological hope that discards what Teilhard sees as the superstition of traditional eschatology:

> We continue from force of habit to think of the Parousia, whereby the Kingdom of God is to be consummated on Earth, as an event of a purely catastrophic nature—that is to say, liable to come about at any moment in history, irrespective of any definite state

23. Teilhard de Chardin, *Future of Man*, 19.
24. Teilhard de Chardin, *Future of Man*, 21.
25. Teilhard de Chardin, *Future of Man*, 305.
26. Teilhard de Chardin, *Future of Man*, 264.

of Mankind. But why should we not assume, in accordance with the latest scientific view of Mankind in a state of anthropogenesis, that the parousiac spark can, of a physical and organic necessity, only be kindled between Heaven and a Mankind which has biologically reached a certain critical evolutionary point of collective maturity?[27]

This "realm of the ultra-human" is one where human beings organize themselves into a unified and rationally ordered global collective, "by developing and embracing on earth, to the utmost extent, all the powers of common vision and unanimisation that are available to us."[28] There are "higher states to be achieved by struggle," for "Mankind as an organic and organized whole" is the basis of what Teilhard calls his "faith in Man."[29]

Teilhard's eschatological vision makes "the collective consummation of earthly Mankind" a "pre-condition" of the kingdom of God; the "eventual biological success of Man on Earth" is an "act of faith" in the coming of that kingdom.[30] And yet, as he describes in more detail in *The Phenomenon of Man*, this is a future that depends on a very particular program of political acts. In one notable and revealing passage he writes,

> The science of man is the practical and theoretical science of hominization. It means profound study of the past and of origins. But still more, it means constructive experiment pursued on a continually renewed object. The programme is immense and its only end or aim is that of the future. . . . So far we have certainly allowed our race to develop at random, and we have given too little thought to the question of what medical and moral factors must replace the crude forces of natural selection should we suppress them. In the course of the coming centuries it is indispensable that a nobly human form of eugenics, on a standard worthy of our personalities, should be discovered and developed.
>
> Eugenics applied to individuals leads to eugenics applied to society . . . Reflective substance requires reflective treatment. If there is a future for mankind, it can only be imagined in terms of a harmonious conciliation of what is free with what is planned and totalized. Points involved are: the distribution of the resources of the globe; the control of the trek towards unpopulated areas; the optimum use of the powers set free by mechanization; the

27. Teilhard de Chardin, *Future of Man*, 267.
28. Teilhard de Chardin, *Future of Man*, 280.
29. Teilhard de Chardin, *Future of Man*, 185.
30. Teilhard de Chardin, *Future of Man*, 237.

physiology of nations and races; geo-economy, geo-politics, geo-demography; the organization of research developing into a reasoned organization of the earth. Whether we like it or not, all the signs and all our needs converge in the same direction. We need and are irresistibly being led to create, by means of and beyond all physics, all biology and all psychology, a science of human energetics.[31]

For Teilhard, humanity as the object of faith is also humanity that must be controlled and improved *en masse*, as a precondition of its eventual unification in the divine Omega Point.[32]

The future depends on the improvement of human beings as a population. This future also depends on the necessary sacrifice of some individuals for the good of the whole. In Teilhard's account, the sacrifices of human beings are mapped onto the sacrifice of Christ, such that those sacrifices are also needed for atonement. "Everything that becomes," he writes, "suffers or sins. The truth about our position in this world is that in it we are on a cross."[33] Please note, for Teilhard, human suffering is not merely an inexplicable tragedy of the fall. Rather, human suffering is necessary for human progress, turning the "great mass of debris" of suffering into "a store of treasure." The "most effective means of progress," he contends, is "to make use of suffering, ghastly and revolting though it be."[34]

The utility of suffering extends to death itself, in which "the soul has offered and surrendered itself to all the great currents of nature."[35] This, too, is guided by divine providence for the progress of creation towards its *telos*. Death "surrenders us totally to God," and in return humans are to "surrender ourselves to death with absolute love and self-abandonment . . . to the domination and guidance of God.[36] For Teilhard, death is to be welcomed as a relief from the bondage of time, which is a constraint and threat rather than a gift:

> Blessed be relentless time and the unending thralldom in which it holds us: the inexorable bondage of time that goes too slowly and

31. Teilhard de Chardin, *Phenomenon of Man*, 282–83.

32. For more on the eugenic aspects of Teilhard's thought, see Slattery, "Dangerous Tendencies of Cosmic Theology," 69–82.

33. Teilhard de Chardin, *On Suffering*, 2.

34. Teilhard de Chardin, *On Suffering*, 3–4.

35. Teilhard de Chardin, *On Suffering*, 5.

36. Teilhard de Chardin, *On Suffering*, 7–9.

frets our impatience, of time that goes too quickly and ages us, of time that never stops and never returns. Blessed, above all, be death and the horror of falling back into the cosmic forces. At the moment of its coming a power as strong as the universe pounces upon our bodies to grind them to dust and dissolve them, and an attraction more tremendous than any material tension draws our unresisting souls towards their proper centre.[37]

There is no distinction in Teilhard's thought between revelation and natural processes, such that the latter is both the site and the culmination of the former. As he writes, "The Christian history of salvation is the conclusion and final summit in the total development of life. In the end, the history of life itself appears to be the history of salvation in its most universal sense in which, and through which, God reveals himself."[38]

This conflation of science and theology, through a conflation of nature and revelation, is a persistent temptation for Christians wishing to make the faith relevant and unthreatening to authorities that treasure scientific expertise as a marker of their own legitimacy. It is as true in contemporary retrievals of his thought as it was in the nineteenth century. Writing on Teilhard, German theologian and Sturmabteilung member Ernst Benz contrasted what he saw as a positive and world-affirming theology with the pessimism and self-questioning that characterized Kierkegaard:

> A new generation has emerged today, which is getting tired of having its life poisoned by people like Kierkegaard, whose human failure and insufficiency for life drove them into devious dialectics. They have discovered that the 'revolt' by which everything real is being questioned has become an empty formula and is, therefore, not credible. It is just used as an element of literary style by intellectuals who have long ago become bourgeois. With profound gratitude, they turn to thinkers who open their hearts for the beauty of the world and humanity.[39]

I will turn to Kierkegaard himself in a few pages, but first a few words are in order about a false response to the thought and the politics represented by these globalized and progressive theologies of the future. In rejecting the one, it is crucial not to embrace the other.

---

37. Teilhard de Chardin, *On Suffering*, 22–23.
38. Benz, *Evolution and Christian Hope*, 159.
39. Benz, *Evolution and Christian Hope*, 227.

The Permutations of Reaction

Liberal narratives of progress have predominated in the first decades of the twenty-first century. These narratives have been contested not only by more traditional forms of conservatism, but also by several new instantiations of reactionary thought. One instance of this can be found in what is often called the neoreaction or "Dark Enlightenment" movement, after the title of an influential essay by British philosopher Nick Land. This loosely connected intellectual current espouses a vision of the future in which technology gives birth to new forms of nondemocratic government, and indeed to a new humanity. While it could be easily dismissed as a fringe movement with few adherents, this strand of conversation in the United States is important for several reasons. First, neoreaction (often called NRx by its proponents) has found considerable support in the information technology industry. This is a telling illustration of the failure of moral formation in engineering as a profession, in which technical expertise is mistaken for wisdom and moral authority. More than that, however, it provides a clear and helpful example of the disruption of the Western secular liberal consensus under the aspect of the demonic, rather than the christological.

Where the disruption that is God in Christ gives humans freedom for love and solidarity based on equality before God, NRx offers a brutal hierarchy of domination achieved through self-transcendence. Land's vision of the future is one in which "there are only two basic human types populating this planet."[40] In this technocratic utopia, "there are autistic nerds, who alone are capable of participating effectively in the advanced technological processes that characterize the emerging economy, and there is everybody else."[41] The process of "assortative mating" between an "explicitly superior" and "genetically self-filtering elite," he writes, leads to a "class-structured" form of "neo-speciation" that is "hyper-racial."[42] This elite will become a new species, as "humanity (and not only society) is coming apart, on an axis whose inferior pole is refuse."[43]

Another leading figure in the neoreactionary movement is Curtis Yarvin, a programmer who writes under the pseudonym Mencius Moldbug. While Yarvin may not share Land's explicitly transhumanist vision,

---

40. O'Connell, "Techno-Libertarians Praying for Dystopia," para. 3.

41. O'Connell, "Techno-Libertarians Praying for Dystopia," para. 3.

42. Land, "Hyper-Racism," para. 7.

43. Land, "Hyper-Racism," para. 7.

his project also prescribes rule by a technological elite. The website of one group associated with his theories, the Hestia Society, explains their program for national restoration succinctly:

> The core of our problem is that there is no one with the secure authority to fix things. The core of our solution is to find a man, and put him in charge, with a real chain of command, and a clear ownership structure. Real leadership would undertake a proper corporate restructuring of [the U.S. government]: Pardon and retire all employees of the old regime; regularize international relations as explicitly either imperial or non-interventionist; nationalize and restructure the banks, media, and universities; and begin the long slow process of organic cultural recovery from centuries of dysfunction.[44]

Yarvin has suggested in an interview with *Vox* writer Dylan Matthews that Elon Musk would be an ideal CEO-monarch of this disrupted and rebooted America.[45] He offers his readers a process of "disillusion" with liberal modernity, the ultimate Matrix-like "true red-hot pill of sodium metal—now igniting in your duodenum" of an "ultimate ascent" into "the glorious air of pure unfiltered reason."[46] Unsurprisingly, Yarvin's ascent is only for the few. Meanwhile, he draws heavily on Thomas Carlyle to argue that some races are more suited for slavery than others.[47]

The temporal vision of this project is one that leaves a trajectory of progress in place while separating it from the political ideals of equality and democracy that at least ostensibly are present in its historically liberal permutations. Technological progress is severed from moral and social progress. The Dark Enlightenment carries the logic of the previous sections (and, indeed, the previous chapter) to its conclusion. Some will flourish. Others will necessarily suffer to enable that flourishing. There are no individuals in this neoreactionary schema (aside from the individual reading the text)—only classes, races, and states. As Australian historian Jonathan Ratcliffe has suggested, neoreactionism accurately accuses liberals of millenarianism while proposing an even more millenarian alternative.[48]

---

44. Gray, "Behind the Internet's Anti-Democracy Movement," paras. 17–18.
45. Matthews, "Alt-Right Explained."
46. Yarvin, "Gentle Introduction to Unqualified Reservations," paras. 2, 3.
47. Yarvin, "Why Carlyle Matters."
48. Ratcliffe, "Return of the Reactionary, Part II."

The Dark Enlightenment is not the only form of reactionary thought to emerge in the last decade, or to inspire the various movements that have coalesced under the banner of the alt-right. There is also a stream of thought that explicitly rejects narratives of progress for a cyclical account of time. At least one instantiation of it has found favor in the spheres of American political influence. This, too, is worth examining in detail—both due to its presence in contemporary political discourse and because as this chapter goes forward, I must take pains to emphasize that my theological argument is saying something quite different.

This cyclical version of reactionary thought has been embraced, most notably, by former White House advisor Stephen K. Bannon. As described in the previously mentioned 1997 work of popular historians Neil Howe and William Strauss, *The Fourth Turning*, a theory of cyclical time on the national and social scale has become influential in the current shaping of the American future. According to Strauss and Howe, American history unfolds within a series of 80-year cycles with four "turnings" characterized by differing relationships between individuals and institutions which in their account constitute the two poles of society, moving through "history's seasonal rhythm of growth, maturation, entropy, and destruction."[49]

In recent American history, the latest and current cycle began with the optimism of the postwar period and continued with the upheavals of the 1960s and 1970s. Strauss and Howe identify the latest third turning as the "Culture Wars" that "began with Reagan's mid-1980's Morning in America" and characterized "an era of national drift and institutional decay."[50] The fourth stage in the cycle was predicted to begin in 2005, and recent interpretations of their work have identified the 2008 financial crisis as the dawn of the period.[51] Winter is not only coming for the followers of this stream of thought, it has already arrived.

Strauss and Howe contend that in such a crisis as the United States will soon enter, or has already now entered, the cohesion of the social body must take precedence in the moral order. This is a period in which "great worldly perils boil off the clutter and complexity of life" and leave only "one simple imperative," that "the society must prevail."[52] This, they argue, requires "a solid public consensus, aggressive institutions, and personal

49. Strauss and Howe, *Fourth Turning*, 3.
50. Strauss and Howe, *Fourth Turning*, 3.
51. Strauss and Howe, *Fourth Turning*, 3.
52. Strauss and Howe, *Fourth Turning*, 103.

sacrifice."[53] The conditions they describe, or prescribe, for the renewal of society are a return to authoritative leadership and moral order. They write that in a crisis period,

> People support new efforts to wield public authority, whose perceived successes soon justify more of the same. Government governs, community obstacles are removed, and laws and customs that resisted change for decades are swiftly shunted aside. A grim preoccupation with civic peril causes spiritual curiosity to decline. A sense of public urgency contributes to a clampdown on bad conduct or antisocial lifestyles. People begin feeling shameful about what they did to absolve guilt. Public order tightens, private risk taking abates, and crime and substance abuse decline. Families strengthen, gender distinctions widen, and child rearing reaches a smothering degree of protection and structure. The young focus their energy on worldly achievements, leaving values in the hands of the old. Wars are fought with fury and for maximum result.[54]

In these times of crisis, as society continues to evolve in oscillating temporal "spirals" of both progress and decline, individual sacrifice is necessary for the good of the social body.[55] Under such a system, death becomes a nutrient for the future growth of the nation. Strauss and Howe write,

> Try to unlearn the linear need to judge change by one-dimensional standards of progress . . . nature neither guarantees progress nor precludes it. . . Try to unlearn the obsessive fear of death (and the anxious quest for death avoidance) that pervades linear thinking in nearly every society. The ancients knew that, without periodic decay and death, nature cannot complete its full round of biological and social change. Without plant death, weeds would strangle the forest. Without human death, memories would never die, and unbroken customs and habits would strangle civilization. Social institutions require no less. Just as floods replenish soils and fires rejuvenate forests, a Fourth Turning clears out society's exhausted elements and creates an opportunity for fresh growth.[56]

In their combination of social science and generational theory, Strauss and Howe generate a clear prescription for societal renewal through cataclysmic struggle—and, indeed, through death. In order for the social body to

53. Strauss and Howe, *Fourth Turning*, 103.

54. Strauss and Howe, *Fourth Turning*, 104.

55. Strauss and Howe, *Fourth Turning*, 105.

56. Strauss and Howe, *Fourth Turning*, 21.

live, the parts of that body deemed superfluous must necessarily be win-
nowed away.

The temporal schematic that Strauss and Howe propose is based on
a rejection of linear time, replacing it with a cycle that exists for its own
sake. Drawing on the work of philosopher of religion Mircea Eliade, they
propose an account of cyclical time that is, they contend, a more primitive—and thus more authentic—way for humans to understand their
temporal existence.[57] They trace the movement towards a linear, progressive understanding of time to the earliest Christians who "tried to root
out calendrical paganism, denounced classical cycles, and pushed under-
ground entire branches of nonlinear learning, such as the hermetic fields of
alchemy and astrology."[58] They see an echo of the eternal, universal pattern
of return in "the core Christian ritual" of "the yearly celebration of a dying
and reborn savior," which "resembles the regenerative midwinter rituals of
the archaic religions."[59] Here, liturgical time functions as an example of a
broader temporal paradigm that does not need the body of that savior in
order to be true. For Strauss and Howe, it is the return itself that matters. In
fact, they close the text with an allusion to the "eternal return" of Nietzsche
paired with a citation of Ecclesiastes.[60] To everything there may be a season,
but here the purpose is a project of national renewal through struggle, and
providence has been collapsed into a vision of American destiny.

The Fullness of Time

Are utopian visions of progress and projects of reaction the only possible
options? The American political and social imagination, both within and
beyond the church, seems captive to that binary. As in the last chapter, a
reading of Kierkegaard may offer a helpful word to the contrary. A reading
of *Fear and Trembling* together with *Philosophical Fragments* can provide
a countervailing witness to both a totalizing account of progress and a reactionary appeal to generalized temporal cycles or an eternal return. Particularly helpful are Kierkegaard's warnings against an appeal to progress,
his Christ-centered, grace-given vision of repetition, and his consistent
attention to the irreplaceability of each "single individual" standing before

57. Strauss and Howe, *Fourth Turning*, 10.
58. Strauss and Howe, *Fourth Turning*, 10.
59. Strauss and Howe, *Fourth Turning*, 10.
60. Strauss and Howe, *Fourth Turning*, 329.

God and in loving relationship with their neighbors. This account of human existence in relationship with God, and with others, offers a different trajectory than either extreme described in the previous section. Christian life in community is life otherwise, neither atomized individualism nor a totalizing vision in which individuals may be sacrificed to secure the future social good.

Writing in *Fear and Trembling*, Kierkegaard's pseudonym Johannes de Silentio reveals something of his true motives in the concluding pages of the text. Taking aim at Hegel's schematic of the progressive unfolding of history and human development, he writes,

> Whatever one generation learns from another, no generation learns the essentially human from a previous one. In this respect, each generation begins primitively, has no task other than what each previous generation had, nor does it advance further, insofar as the previous generations did not betray the task and deceive themselves. . . . But the highest passion in a person is faith, and here no generation begins at any other point than where the previous one did. Each generation begins all over again; the next generation advances no further than the previous one, that is, if that one was faithful to the task and did not leave it high and dry. That it should be fatiguing is, of course, something that one generation cannot say, for the generation does indeed have the task and has nothing to do with the fact that the previous generation had the same task, unless this particular generation, or the individuals in it, presumptuously assumes the place that belongs to the spirit who rules the world and who has the patience not to become weary.[61]

De Silentio is clear in the end that the "urge to go further" is "an old story in the world," yet in his confusion earlier in the text he also reveals another problematic aspect of theologies that would make ushering in the kingdom of God a matter for human, not divine, agency.

This is a question with soteriological as well as eschatological significance. God's saving work in Christ, and the way that saving is accomplished, does not change. Rhetoric will come and go. Philosophies will wax and wane. Administrations right or left will be in or out of the White House. Through it all, salvation in Christ—both now and in the age to come—arrives as sheer, wondrous gift, and not from within humanity.

The gift is not ours to grasp, no matter how strong the temptation to think we can propel ourselves into faith and save ourselves in the process,

---

61. Kierkegaard, *Fear and Trembling*, 121–22.

no matter how much we would like to generate ourselves rather than be born anew by another. Writing in *Fear and Trembling*, De Silentio invites his readers to see themselves as knights of faith, and to envision the (in)famous "leap" of faith as a heroic act that is possible through human effort.[62] But as Kierkegaard, writing in the voice of De Silentio, makes clear in a footnote, these are merely temptations that do not take into account human sin and the depth to which salvation comes as a gift and not as an achievement:

> Up until now I have assiduously avoided any reference to the question of sin and its reality [Realitet]. The whole work is centered on Abraham, and I can still encompass him in immediate categories—that is, insofar as I can understand him. As soon as sin emerges, ethics founders precisely on repentance; for repentance is the highest ethical expression, but precisely as such it is the deepest ethical self-contradiction.[63]

Any optimism about the sufficiency of human effort to propel us towards God runs aground on the reality of sin and our need for a savior. Louise Carroll Keeley suggests that, in drawing on the story of Tobias and Sarah in the book of Tobit, De Silentio reveals something of the truth within his misunderstandings of faith.[64] Rather than being a matter of "self-procreation," humanity's future is secured through gratuitous sacrifice, a gift so extravagant that we can hardly bear to receive it:[65]

> Tobias behaves gallantly and resolutely and chivalrously, but any man who does not have the courage for that is a milksop who does not know what love is or what it is to be a man or what is worth living for; he has not even grasped the little mystery that it is better to give than to receive and has no intimation of the great mystery that it is far more difficult to receive than to give, that is, if one has had the courage to do without and in the hour of distress did not prove a coward. No, Sarah is the heroic character. She is the one I want to approach as I have never approached any girl or been tempted in thought to approach anyone of whom I have read. For what love for God it takes to be willing to let oneself be healed when from the very beginning one in all innocence has been botched, from the very beginning has been a damaged specimen

62. Kierkegaard, *Fear and Trembling*, 36.
63. Kierkegaard, *Fear and Trembling*, 98–99.
64. Keeley, "Parables of Problem III," 127–54.
65. Keeley, "Parables of Problem III," 101.

of a human being! What ethical maturity to take upon oneself the responsibility of permitting the beloved to do something so hazardous! What humility before another person! What faith in God that she would not in the very next moment hate the man to whom she owed everything![66]

The motif of self-procreation, of giving birth to oneself, is a consistent target of Kierkegaard's critique. It appears in *Either/Or*, as Judge William takes the bourgeois logic of the self-made man to its logical—and heretical—conclusion, making self-knowledge the means by which "the individual is made pregnant by himself and gives birth to himself."[67] It appears as well in *Philosophical Fragments*, where Johannes Climacus contrasts what he dubs "the Socratic" search for truth with the gift of Jesus Christ.

In the Socratic, he writes, "every human being is himself the midpoint, and the whole world focuses only on him because his self-knowledge is God-knowledge."[68] The truth is brought forth from within the learner, where it already resides:

> [T]he ultimate idea in all questioning is that the person asked must himself possess the truth and acquire it by himself. The temporal point of departure is a nothing, because in the same moment I discover that I have known the truth from eternity without knowing it, in the same instant that moment is hidden in the eternal, assimilated into it in such a way that I, so to speak, still cannot find it even if I were to look for it, because there is no Here and no There, but only an *ubique et nusquam* [everywhere and nowhere].[69]

Contrasted with this moment that is not a moment at all, because it is "everywhere and nowhere," Climacus suggests a "moment" that has "decisive significance," which is none other than the saving moment of Jesus Christ.[70] In this moment, time is fulfilled, and human beings receive the time that is given to them. He writes,

> A moment such as this is unique. To be sure, it is short and temporal, as the moment is; it is passing, as the moment is, past, as the moment is in the next moment, and yet it is decisive, and yet it is

---

66. Kierkegaard, *Fear and Trembling*, 103–4.

67. Kierkegaard, *Either/Or II*, 259.

68. Kierkegaard, *Philosophical Fragments*, 11.

69. Kierkegaard, *Philosophical Fragments*, 13.

70. Kierkegaard, *Philosophical Fragments*, 28.

filled with the eternal. A moment such as this must have a special name. Let us call it: the fullness of time.[71]

As noted in the previous chapter, this moment is not a matter of a gradual ascent towards truth, or a process of becoming what already resides within creation. Instead, it "must be attempted by a descent," which is the coming of the Word made flesh in the form of a servant.[72]

As the moment of the incarnation, this moment is unique and singular, but at the same time it presents itself to each believer just as it did to the first disciples. This repetition is something other than the generalized temporal cycle that we find in the work of Eliade, or indeed in the concept of the eternal return suggested by Nietzsche. What is repeated is of first importance, and the fact of the repetition is that which makes Christ accessible to each generation—to each "single individual"—in faith.

Climacus points towards how this is possible in a brief section entitled "Interlude," in which he compares the situation of the believer at firsthand (the disciples of Jesus) with contemporary Christians and asks "is the past more necessary than the future?"[73] Writing in a time when Christianity itself had been placed within what Paul Holmer calls the Hegelian "moving stair that human history is supposed to be," Kierkegaard rejects any attempt to read necessity into any past event, including the event of Jesus Christ.[74]

Christian faith, and Christ himself, cannot be subsumed under a project for societal improvement or the progressive unfolding of all creation. It is a gift of sovereign freedom and not a matter of necessity, once given in history and given again and again to each believer. This is the repetition of which Kierkegaard writes, and as such it cannot be generalized into a cyclical pattern for the sake of the pattern itself. It was "not necessary when it came into existence" and "no more necessary as future than it is necessary as past.[75] Is there a difference between the first-century believer and one in nineteenth-century Denmark? For Kierkegaard, the answer is no, because each believer, each single individual, repeats the act of faith for herself.

Crucially, Kierkegaard also seems to suggest in the interlude that Christ encounters each believer in free grace through repeated means that

71. Kierkegaard, *Philosophical Fragments*, 18.

72. Kierkegaard, *Philosophical Fragments*, 31.

73. Kierkegaard, *Philosophical Fragments*, 72.

74. Holmer, *On Kierkegaard and the Truth*, 26; Kierkegaard, *Philosophical Fragments*, 79–80.

75. Kierkegaard, *Philosophical Fragments*, 88.

present themselves directly to the senses. Throughout the section, he repeats the refrain, "immediate sensation and cognition cannot deceive."[76] As
Amy Laura Hall has suggested in her reading of *Philosophical Fragments*,
the act by which each "single individual" receives grace—and themselves—
as a gift is a matter of sacramental presence rather than of intellectual
comprehension.[77] This is a matter that depends constantly and entirely on
God's action. Climacus writes that "the whole thing is in suspense" and
"built upon the abyss," such that it is "not to be passed on like real estate"
but rather "handed down to the single individual only under the agreement
that it is by virtue of a paradox."[78]

Finally, for Kierkegaard, Christianity is a matter that addresses itself
to the "single individual," to whom is then addressed the divine commandment to love the neighbor. Salvation is not a collective process in which the
individual is obscured, or, at worst, treated as expendable. Kierkegaard is
not proposing a form of individualism, in which an atomized and autono-
mous subject has no need for her neighbors. As *Works of Love* makes clear,
and as the next chapter will discuss in more depth, Christianity cannot exist without the love of the neighbor, without the particularity of concrete
human relationships. Rather, he reminds us that currently existing human
beings cannot be thought of as expendable sacrifices in a project to secure
the future. Jürgen Moltmann's appraisal of Teilhard de Chardin succinctly
diagnoses this problem:

> Evolution always means selection. Many living things are sacrificed
> in order that "the fittest"—which means the most effective and the
> most adaptable—may survive. In this way higher and increasingly
> complex life systems, which can react to changed environments,
> undoubtedly develop. But in the same process milliards of living
> things fall by the wayside and disappear into evolution's rubbish
> bin. Evolution is not merely a constructive affair on nature's part.
> It is a cruel one too. It is a kind of biological execution of the Last
> Judgment on the weak, the sick and the "unfit."[79]

Human beings are not, and cannot be, the substrate upon which the kingdom of God is built.[80] To claim otherwise is to place oneself in the position

76. Kierkegaard, *Philosophical Fragments*, 81.
77. Hall and Slade, "Single Individual in Ordinary Time," 66–82.
78. Hall and Slade, "Single Individual in Ordinary Time," 75.
79. Moltmann, *Way of Jesus Christ*, 294.
80. Moltmann, *Way of Jesus Christ*, 297.

of transparency, as one who stands outside the laws of nature as the victor while others are subject to both selection and domination.

His Eternity for Our Future

Karl Barth did not live to complete the planned volume(s) on eschatology in the *Church Dogmatics*. Yet in other places throughout the text, his work has much to say on the future of creation as it is bound up in, and determined by, the person and work of Jesus Christ. Both in the doctrine of creation and the doctrine of reconciliation, he addresses the future in ways that witness against either anxiety or despair, and that counter arguments like those of Teilhard de Chardin that place the future of creation within creation itself. Moreover, he also clearly argues against attempts to make repetition or cyclical time an end in itself or a generalized pattern within which Christ is an example of some broader truth.

Writing in the paragraph on the doctrine of providence in *Church Dogmatics* III/3, Barth engages directly with German evolutionary biologist Ernst Haeckel. Here, Barth argues against any notion that divine providence works itself out from within creation. The future of the creature in the sense of its preservation is assured by a constant and free act of God, rather than from any property of the creature itself. As he argues, the preserving act of God cannot be thought of as mediated by the presence of natural laws—including that of evolution. He writes, "the identification of the divine preservation with the creaturely nexus means a flat denial of the fact that this nexus is not grounded upon or maintained by itself, but has over it an independent Lord and Sustainer." It is "a poor expedient when all that the religious understanding can do is to interpret as an act of divine preservation that which otherwise would have to be regarded merely as the foundation and preservation of the world by itself."[81]

In other words, God does not preserve the creature's future merely in the sense of a divine watchmaker who sets creation in motion in accordance with physical laws. Instead, even those things considered "natural" owe their life-preserving power to the constant action of the Word:

> Nothing is more natural for the sun than to rise day after day, and yet it is God who causes it to rise (Mt. 5:45). And this is how we have to understand Matthew 4:4 ("Man doth not live by bread alone"): Even bread has no power to nourish in the sense that it

81. Barth, *Church Dogmatics* III/3, 66.

could do so apart from the Word of God by which it was created and has its power to nourish, but in order to exercise this property it needs the continual influence (*influxus*) of the creative and sustaining Word of God. Similarly neither herbs and prepared medicines nor the physician who administers them can of themselves and as such heal a man, but only the hand of God present within them. In short, even in the indirectness in which it is undoubtedly fulfilled, the preservation of the creature must still be regarded as an action of God as He freely disposes of the whole mediation of the creature, an action which is not conditioned by this mediation but on the contrary conditions it.[82]

Creation, and creatures including humanity, are neither self-narrating, self-consituting, or self-preserving. Instead, the hand of God sustains and preserves creation even within creaturely means.

Turning now to the question of cyclical time that exists in itself, we find in the first volume of the doctrine of reconciliation that Barth distinguishes clearly between that which can be thought of in terms of repetition and that which cannot. The events of cross and resurrection establish a basic irreversibility and unrepeatability into time:

> It is rather like a one-way street. It cannot be reversed. The crucifixion and death of Jesus Christ took place once. As this happening once it stands eternally before God and it is the basis and truth of the alteration of the human situation willed and brought about by God: from sin to righteousness, from captivity to freedom, from lying to truth, from death to life, our conversion to Him. For that reason the crucifixion and death of Jesus Christ does not ever take place again. But the life of the Resurrected as the life of the Crucified, as it began in that Easter period, and needs no new beginning, is an eternal life, a life which is also continuous in time.[83]

As he continues, he points out the ways that even Kierkegaard can be misinterpreted to make Christianity a matter of eternal cycles:

> The way of God the Father, Son and Holy Spirit, the way of the true God, is not a cycle, a way of eternal recurrence, in which the end is a constant beginning. It is the way of myth which is cyclic, an eternal recurrence, summoning man to endless repetitions, to that eternal oscillation between Yes and No, grace and judgment, life and death. We must not mythologise the Gospel of the way of the

82. Barth, *Church Dogmatics* III/3, 67.
83. Barth, *Church Dogmatics* IV/1, 343.

true God (not even in the name of Kierkegaard or Luther himself). We must not interpret it in terms of a cycle. We must not make the Christian life and theological thinking and the Church's preaching and instruction and pastoral care like the ox which is bound to a stake and, driven by the owner's whip, has to trot round and round turning the wheel. We must not violently make of Christianity a movement of reaction and think that we can force it on the world in this form. God has rejected from all eternity. He has condemned and judged and put to death in time. He has put all to death in a Son who obediently willed to suffer death in the place of all. And He never comes back to this point. He never begins here. And in faith, in gratitude, in obedience, in the knowledge of His way, we ourselves can only be prevented from beginning here. . . . And the *telos* of the way which He has gone in the person and work, in the history of Jesus Christ, is our beginning-His electing, therefore. His love, His saving, His making alive.[84]

In short, the unrepeatable, once-for-all nature of cross and resurrection introduces a direction into time, but not as a trajectory of progress. Instead, it means Christ cannot be collapsed into an example of a more generalized cyclical concept of time. The cycle is not the defining feature of time. Jesus Christ is.

Progressive thinkers like Rauschenbusch and Teilhard de Chardin share with the representatives of neoreaction the tendency to elide any human being—whether you, me, a child we love, a parent we remember, or a neighbor we do not understand—in favor of the social body as a whole. Here, too, Barth can contribute a contrary word. There is an irreducible duality in human relationships, just as there are between the creature and God: the duality of I and Thou addressing each other. Daring the vulnerability involved in "letting ourselves be seen and not unseen by one another" is a step in being human that "cannot be replaced by the exercise of any human capacity or virtue."[85] Any other basis for human relationship risks the tyranny of bureaucracy, creating a path of inhumanity for human relationships, "the encounter of the blind with those whom they treat as blind."[86] As he explains,

> Where a man thinks he sees and knows a group, or a group a man, or one group another group, ambiguity always arises. After all, it

84. Barth, *Church Dogmatics* IV/1, 345.
85. Barth, *Church Dogmatics* III/2, 251.
86. Barth, *Church Dogmatics* III/2, 252.

might be only a matter of psychology and not the other man, of pedagogics and not the child, of sociological statistics and systematisation and not the individual, of the general and not the particular, which is the only thing that really counts in this respect. This is the dangerous—and usually more than dangerous—limit of all planning and philanthropy, but also of all doctrine and instruction, of all politics, and especially of all socialism. Whether on the one side or the other or both there is maintained or broken a closed and blind existence, thinking and speaking in the group, whether the one concrete man is invisible or visible to the other concrete man, is what decides whether there is humanity in all this or not. Bureaucracy is the form in which man participates with his fellows when this first step into mutual openness is not taken, and not taken because duality is evaded for the sake of the simplicity of a general consideration and a general programme.[87]

The bureaucratization of human beings into a collective social body to be variously redeemed or restored *en masse*, particularly through the necessary suffering or death of some members of the social body, is a feature shared by both the scientific progressivism and technological reactionary currents described earlier in the chapter. In both cases, however, the key duality of relationship between one concrete and particular human being and another is blurred or erased.

Unsurprisingly, the sections in the doctrine of creation that address creaturely existence in time are perhaps the most directly relevant to human anxieties for the future. Writing on "Given Time," Barth connects fear for the future with an inability to grapple with the past. It is "in memory" that humans "start with an awareness of the problematical character of our being in the present and therefore in the future as well."[88] The result, he suggests, is either a flight into the past or a search for the oblivion promised by progress, in which everything is sheer futurity. To take recourse into nostalgia is a well-worn path, especially within theological thought. And yet it is revealed as a problem and not a solution. Barth writes, "when a man regrets to-day and has no hope for to-morrow, he has recourse to memory. And when the same thing happens to a whole generation, it resorts to historicism, romantically or scientifically investigating what was."[89] This is the route of Big History, in which an account of origins determines

87. Barth, *Church Dogmatics* III/2, 252.
88. Barth, *Church Dogmatics* III/2, 534.
89. Barth, *Church Dogmatics* III/2, 534.

the meaning of human life. But it is also the trajectory of writers like Strauss and Howe who would plumb the history of the nation-state for carefully curated markers of its destiny.

If the retreat into history is an idolatry of memory for Barth, faith in progress is a flight into oblivion. Here, he writes, "we start from the opposite end."[90] As he eloquently explains,

> We flee from the cathedrals, prisons, inns and catacombs where we were yesterday, into the light of to-day with its promise of even greater light to-morrow. When we try, consciously or unconsciously, to forget the past, we simply let it lie to the extent that it is not absorbed into the present. . . . When a man cannot be happy about the past, he seeks happiness in the present and future. And when a whole generation finds it impossible to make sense of the past, it glories all the more readily in the "spirit of the age," that is, of its own age, and succumbs to the belief in progress. This too, as we know, can be partially successful. When we are tired of our old letters and diaries we can tear them up and burn them. We can suppress all that we were and experienced and said and did. We can replace it by a picture of what we think we can and should be and experience and say and do now and in the future, finding freedom and beginning life all over again, and this time real life in the admiration and service which it evokes. But again our real intention eludes us. Our being in the present and future is not a secure refuge from the problems of the past. We can paint rosy pictures of our being in the present, but these pictures bear no relation to the reality which is just as problematical as our being in the past. It is as foolish to flee from Scylla to Charybdis as vice versa.[91]

Humanity is not trapped between the false allure of memory and the equally false promise of a utopian future of its own making. Because Jesus Christ has taken on time, and because he is the Lord of time, creaturely time is embraced in God's eternity and returned to humanity as gift. Christology is the ground for anthropology in respect to time, an anthropology of humanity "under and with God in his time," existing "with the one Jesus (as the recipient of the divine promise addressed to him in the man Jesus) in the time created and given" by God.[92]

90. Barth, *Church Dogmatics* III/2, 535.
91. Barth, *Church Dogmatics* III/2, 535.
92. Barth, *Church Dogmatics* III/2, 552–53.

As the time of God, the time of Jesus is not "confined to the three dimensions" of beginning, duration, and end. "The all-inclusive 'I am' rules out any notion that the three dimensions, past, present, and future, simply follow each other in succession."[93] Instead, they are simultaneous, but in a complex way that follows a Trinitarian logic. In the time of Jesus, the yesterday, today, and forever, the was, is, and is to come, coinhere perichoretically. This temporal complexity is not only astonishing in its own right, but it also prevents any attempt to linearize Jesus into a preconceived notion of time, or to collapse the future into an account of human progress.

Finally, Barth reminds readers that a Christian eschatology can never be a disembodied eschatology, and that the kingdom of God comes in the body of Jesus Christ and not through human effort, either outside the church or within it. The expectation of Christ as the "concrete form" of the Christian hope, and in particular as the once-and-future hope of Advent, occasions in us the same "patient joy" and "joyful patience," the same "holy impatience and holy patience" as it did in the first Christians.[94] The time of Jesus Christ is not limited to the past and present, with the past "prolonged into and determining" that present as necessary prior stages in a trajectory of development.[95] As Barth explains, to hold otherwise is to fall victim to a form of utopianism that is incompatible with Scripture. In a passage that bears quoting at length in this confused and confusing political moment, he writes,

> Hope would then have meant confidence in the power of the Gospel to cleanse and sanctify the individual and to permeate society. The apostles would have looked forward to a progressive immanent development of the new life opened up by the resurrection, and then of the state of human and creaturely things generally, in the direction of an ideal of good and happy humanity corresponding to the beginning, to be attained approximately in this world and perfectly in a better hereafter, and identifiable with the kingdom of God. Indeed, there have been whole periods in the history of the Church when this version of the Christian hope has been regarded as necessary both in theory and in practice. The New Testament does not contain a single shred of evidence to support this view. Compared with what the New Testament calls hope, this Utopian version can only be described as a fabrication,

93. Barth, *Church Dogmatics* III/2, 465.
94. Barth, *Church Dogmatics* III/2, 492.
95. Barth, *Church Dogmatics* III/2, 486.

however well-meaning and attractive. The salient feature about it is that in the last resort it can do without Jesus. It may know Him as the Jesus of yesterday and to-day, but it knows nothing of Him as . . . the One who comes. [T]he New Testament looks forward, not merely to a better future, but to a future which sets a term to the whole time process, and in its perfection includes and surpasses absolutely all the contents of time. This future will be a wholly new order, quite independent of all creaturely and even Christian development.[96]

In a culture where technological utopianism is ubiquitous, the temptations to offer a Christian counterpart to this thinking are ubiquitous as well. Yet we are called to risk the strangeness of a scriptural eschatology that confesses that in the end, the end is not up to us.

96. Barth, *Church Dogmatics* III/2, 486.

4

Between[1]

While the American Creed is Protestantism without God,
the American civil religion is Christianity without Christ.

—SAMUEL P. HUNTINGTON[2]

Well, I preach the Church Without Christ. I'm member and preacher to that
church where the blind don't see and the lame don't walk and what's dead
stays that way.... I'm going to preach it to whoever'll listen at whatever place.
I'm going to preach there was no Fall because there was nothing to fall from
and no Redemption because there was no Fall and no Judgment because
there wasn't the first two.

—HAZEL MOTES, IN FLANNERY O'CONNOR'S *WISE BLOOD*[3]

Later [Hazel] saw Jesus move from tree to tree in the back of his mind, a
wild ragged figure motioning him to turn around and come off into the dark
where he might be walking on the water and not know it and then suddenly
know it and drown.

—FLANNERY O'CONNOR[4]

1. An edited version of some portions of this chapter also appears as "Kierkegaard
and the Politics of Time," in Sirvent and Morgan, *Kierkegaard and Political Theology*.

2. Huntington, *Who Are We?*, 106.

3. O'Connor, *Wise Blood*, 54.

4. O'Connor, *Wise Blood*, 22.

Just then a lawyer stood up to test Jesus. "Teacher," he said, "what must I do to inherit eternal life?" He said to him, "What is written in the law? What do you read there?" He answered, "You shall love the Lord your God with all your heart, and with all your soul, and with all your strength, and with all your mind; and your neighbor as yourself." And he said to him, "You have given the right answer; do this, and you will live." But wanting to justify himself, he asked Jesus, "And who is my neighbor?"

—LUKE 10:25–29 (NRSV)

"These people are being denuded, stripped, washed out, destroyed. They are being reduced to a state of childish impotence where they have to be taken care of and where they produce nothing."[5] Reading these sentences in isolation, someone who cares about and reads texts about race and class in the US might conclude that they come from a recent popular book on the social and economic plight of present-day Appalachian people. But they do not. These words were written in 1923 by Frank Tannenbaum in a portrait of the textile mill workers of North Carolina. The "mountaineer or small cotton farmer" who moves to the mill village, he writes, is "lost to the community," becoming culturally childish despite their "Anglo-Saxon" heritage that has "given the South and the nation some of their best spiritual leadership."[6] The conditions of mill work and mill life, Tannenbaum writes, have led the people he describes down a temporal trajectory, away from contemporaneity and towards a childish primitivism and moral degeneracy. Despite the fact that "the best blood in the country flows in their veins," they have become decivilized.[7]

The prevalence of this rhetoric of progress and backwardness may suggest it is part of the natural order of things, rather than a political maneuver. But at the heart of this political tactic is a tendency to arrange oneself and one's neighbors on a temporal trajectory, distinguishing one's own place in the present from the supposed primitivity of particular neighbors. That is to say, some people, generally the ones doing the arranging, live in the present day. Others, however, are marked as politically, culturally,

5. Tannenbaum, "South Buries Its Anglo-Saxons," 210.
6. Tannenbaum, "South Buries Its Anglo-Saxons," 210.
7. Tannenbaum, "South Buries Its Anglo-Saxons," 205.

or psychologically backward and mired in the past—or placed outside of history altogether.

This maneuver is not just a matter of theoretical or of historical interest. The politics of temporal separation and distancing that marked Tannenbaum's magazine feature persist into the present day, in venues that range from projects in scientific anthropology to the language of popular political discourse. Using the theoretical insights of anthropologist Johannes Fabian among others, I will show how the politics of time are, at a fundamental level, a problem of soteriology. The questions that lie underneath the impulse to arrange one's neighbors along a temporal continuum are twofold: "Who saves, and by what means?," and "Who is my neighbor?" Yet, the Christian life involves reorienting not just our thought but our selves towards contemporaneity with Christ and with our neighbors. Underlying all politics is the inconvenient and persistent question of the neighbor, who calls into question our own works of love.

We Have Always Been "Coming Apart"

The fear of falling into the past persists into the present day. One example among many in the popular press is the unsubtly titled 2012 book, *Becoming China's Bitch and Nine More Catastrophes We Must Avoid Right Now*. The author, former Goldman Sachs partner and current University of Virginia board member Peter Kiernan, warns of the increasing threat that China poses to American economic and political supremacy. His "Manifesto for the Radical Center" focuses on the "possibility that the U.S. might fall behind China in the economic race to the top, and that we might be dependent on China."[8] Kiernan's prescribed cure for America's economic infirmity is as ambitious as it is encyclopedic, touching briefly on topics that range from stem cell research to immigration reform to Middle East policy. Notably, he devotes significant attention to the role of progress in science and technology, the need to reform a "slipping" educational system filled with "lackadaisical students," and the dangers of religious zeal compared to a more usefully acculturated and contemporary form of civil Christianity.[9] Above all, however, he emphasizes that properly progressive, technocratic

8. Kiernan, *Becoming China's Bitch*, 149.
9. Kiernan, *Becoming China's Bitch*, 330, 334.

leaders are needed to guide and unify the politically "polarized" American population in a rapidly changing globalized context.[10]

Yet these proposals to buttress national vigor in the face of perceived decline are neither unique nor new. Contemporary pundits from the right as well as the technocratic center have variously espoused many of the same ideas. Crucially, their common focus on renewing national vigor through education, the deployment of scientific methodology, and moral renewal has a history. Few texts illustrate the convergence between national anxieties past and present more clearly than Arnold White's 1901 text *Efficiency and Empire*. White, one of the leading advocates of the British National Efficiency movement, proposed a similarly technocratic response to the emergence of the United States and Germany as threats to British imperial supremacy at the turn of the twentieth century.[11] I begin this chapter by tracing some of the threads that connect contemporary discourses on American decline and renewal to those earlier attempts to apply the principles of scientific management to the government of a global power, especially insofar as they describe certain segments of the population to be governed as temporally retrograde.

The Best Men

Written at the height of the Second Boer War, *Efficiency and Empire* was a response to the perceived weakness and incapacity that Britain's struggles in the Transvaal demonstrated to its rivals, particularly to Germany. Arnold White presents a stark ultimatum to his compatriots, warning that "either efficiency must be restored to the British administrative system," or "the decline of the British Empire will date from the first decade of the twentieth century."[12] His solution focuses on replacing the politically minded "rhetoricians" and aristocrats of "smart society" in government with "the best men," selected by a meritocracy of the fittest.[13] Knowledge of the scientific "principles of business methods," as well as the moral vigor to act on them, is thus essential to imperial governance[14]:

---

10. Kiernan, *Becoming China's Bitch*, 5.

11. Searle, *Quest for National Efficiency*, 55.

12. White, *Efficiency and Empire*, 14.

13. White, *Efficiency and Empire*, 105, 242.

14. White, *Efficiency and Empire*, 3.

The key to this moulding of fitness, whether in officials, cows, or pouter pigeons, is man's power of selection. We disobey the unbending law of evolution in the choice of our rulers and higher officials because we do not exert an adequate power of selection, and consequently have not acquired a useful breed of either. Instead of adjusting our practice of obedience to the laws of natural selection, we have inverted them in dealing with our civil and military service. There is little or no struggle for existence in the higher ranks of State servants. They hold office on a freehold tenure. The inefficient members are not ruthlessly destroyed.[15]

White appeals to these Darwinian principles throughout the text, linking the decision-making and administrative skills of "efficient" officials to their sense of scientific objectivity.[16] In addition, he contrasts those virtues with the subjective "sickly emotion" associated with philanthropic charity, Christian mercy, and democratic idealism.[17] As the next section will show, the ramifications of this approach extend far beyond the appointment of civil servants and military commanders. These ruthlessly selected and disciplined officials are expected to make similarly ruthless decisions about the management of the populations they govern.

White suggests that men of action, rather than words, are most suited to govern, in particular those who "now devote themselves to making and working the great railways, organizing fleets of mail steamers, and administering commercial affairs on a great scale."[18] In one chapter title, White asks the rhetorical question, "Should business men rule us?" Over the course of the book, he answers with an unqualified yes.

It is difficult to read this paean to the technocratic future of empire without immediately recalling the writing of Peter Kiernan and his like-minded contemporaries. Like White, Kiernan assumes Darwinian agonism is the underlying logic of human existence. For example, his work on educational reform presupposes "competition plays a role in driving improvement in every field of human endeavor, schooling children included."[19] Education in science is as central to Kiernan's project of national renewal as it was for White, and he also deploys the threat of an authoritarian (and

15. White, *Efficiency and Empire*, 14.
16. White, *Efficiency and Empire*, 23.
17. White, *Efficiency and Empire*, 102.
18. White, *Efficiency and Empire*, 25, 76.
19. Kiernan, *Becoming China's Bitch*, 344.

thus more efficient) foreign regime to emphasize the urgency of change.[20] Kiernan presents his agenda as radically apolitical, a "revolutionary" centrist "movement" for national unity, based on the pragmatic evaluation of data rather than ideological debate.[21] Finally, he is convinced business leaders like himself can solve even the most intractable national woes more effectively than the current elected government. Even in the wake of the economic crisis of 2008, Kiernan believes his colleagues should influence more, not less, of the nation's common life:

> Class-war slurs on Wall Streeters must feel pretty terrific. But the time has come to focus specifically on the few bad guys and let the rest of business get back to doing its job. I must admit, business has a broken brand. Pretty shabby considering we are brand experts. One way we can get our groove back is by taking the right kind of businesslike approach to solving the nation's problems.[22]

Although Kiernan is sufficiently savvy about matters of branding to eschew the language of rule, his answer to White's question, "Should business men rule us?," is also an unqualified yes.

Patches of Barbarianism Within

In *Efficiency and Empire*, White places the figure of the business man at the apex of a trajectory of progress, contrasting it directly with the inefficient and genetically "unfit" members of the population who represent a temporal as well as a financial impediment to national vigor. An enthusiastic proponent of the eugenics movement, he describes the dysgenic threat to imperial efficiency at length and in detail. For the purposes of this chapter, however, the excerpt below is sufficient to convey the flavor of his thought:

> If the nation is to be "graded up," existing sources of degeneracy must be cut off. To do so, society requires not money, but common sense; not heedless pity for individuals, but wise compassion for the race; not emotion, but courage to face ghastly truths. For the present we are safe from attack by barbarians from without. Patches of barbarianism within require not pity but the knife. What can society do to discharge its duty as trustee for posterity, to preserve the vigour of the race, and to raise the practicable

20. Kiernan, *Becoming China's Bitch.*, 347.
21. Kiernan, *Becoming China's Bitch*, xx.
22. Kiernan, *Becoming China's Bitch*, xvi.

ideals of Anglo-Saxons? If we are to become a healthy people, the permanent segregation of habitual criminals, paupers, drunkards, maniacs, and tramps must be deliberately undertaken. Secondly, the marriage law requires overhauling. In England a girl may be married at twelve years of age, and a boy at fourteen. A limit of age suitable to a sub-tropical country does not harmonise with our climate and social conditions. A medical certificate of physical and mental fitness for the marriage state should be exacted by a wise State before union, in the interest of the unborn, who deserve justice no less than their parents deserve compassion.[23]

While several aspects of this passage are noteworthy, the most salient is its description of the unfit as "patches of barbarianism within." This language is a prime example of what Johannes Fabian calls "temporal distancing," in which the denial of coeval existence in time creates the anthropological other as an object.[24]

In *Time and the Other*, a text that deals primarily with the problem of time within anthropological science, Fabian describes a modern shift that involves both temporal and geographic processes tied to secularization. Previously, he argues, time was negotiated in terms of a sacred history, and the determinative temporal framework was the history of salvation based in the specificity and particularity of the incarnation. Modernity, for Fabian, enacts a continual process of secularizing time by not just linearizing, but also by generalizing and universalizing it. He also notes the connection of time and space, as time becomes related to travel in a new way:

> In the Christian tradition, the Savior's and the saints' passages on earth had been perceived as constituent events of a sacred history. To be sure, this had occasioned much travel to foreign parts in the form of pilgrimages, crusades, and missions. But for the established bourgeoisie of the eighteenth century, travel was to become (at least potentially) every man's source of philosophical, secular knowledge. Religious travel had been to the centers of religion, or to the souls to be saved; now, secular travel was from the centers of learning and power to the places where man was to find nothing but himself.[25]

In this form of travel, new people were encountered as a way to write the history of "man." As a result, the temporal was tied to the geographical, time

23. White, *Efficiency and Empire*, 120.
24. Fabian, *Time and the Other*, 75.
25. Fabian, *Time and the Other*, 6.

to space, and in particular to narratives of exploration and discovery. In the words of the eighteenth-century French explorer, the Comte de Lapérouse, "the modern navigators only have one objective when they describe the customs of new peoples: to complete the history of man."[26] This "new science of travel" was inextricably intertwined with "natural-historical projects of observation, collection, and classification."[27]

By linking the temporal and the geographical through these secular, scientific voyages of exploration, the stage would be set for the next shift in anthropological thought. Fabian notes that in the nineteenth century, time became "immanent to," and "coextensive with," the material world or with the idea of "nature."[28] At the same time, relationships between parts of the world were understood as temporal relationships, such that "dispersal in space" indicates "sequence in Time."[29] At the same time as these relationships were presented as objective and universal, however, they reintroduced a covert form of specificity. The histories completed through these scientific voyages were part of a particular story of salvation through travel, discovery, and progress that posits some human beings as temporally atavistic or primitive, while others are destined to bring salvation to them:

> The natural histories of evolutionism reintroduced a kind of specificity of time and place—in fact a history of retroactive salvation—that has its closest counterpart in the Christian-medieval vision contested by the Enlightenment. This was politically all the more reactionary because it pretended to rest on strictly scientific hence universally valued principles. In fact little more had been done than to replace faith in salvation by faith in progress and industry, and the Mediterranean as the hub of history by Victorian England.[30]

Living societies and past cultures were arranged on a continuous temporal slope, in which some were located upstream and others downstream, separated by the temporal rhetoric of "then" and the geographies of "there."[31]

The political tactic of temporal distancing described by Fabian is rooted in what he calls the "denial of coevalness." This is defined as "a persistent

26. Fabian, *Time and the Other*, 8
27. Fabian, *Time and the Other*, 8.
28. Fabian, *Time and the Other*, 11.
29. Fabian, *Time and the Other*, 12.
30. Fabian, *Time and the Other*, 17.
31. Fabian, *Time and the Other*, 27.

and systematic tendency to place the referent(s) of anthropology in a Time other than the present of the producer of anthropological discourse."[32] In the context of exploration and colonialism, this distancing results in what Fabian calls "a kind of political physics," in which "it is impossible for two bodies to occupy the same space at the same time."[33] As the history of colonialism and relations with indigenous peoples tragically reveals, it then becomes logical to either (1) "move or remove the other body," or (2) assign the other body to a different time.[34] In this way, the separation between Western man and the object of anthropological inquiry as well as political subjugation is maintained.

As a colonial technique brought to bear on the population of the metropole, temporal distancing is one way of manipulating the "political physics" of bodies in time and space:

> When in the course of colonial expansion a Western body came to occupy, literally, the space of an autochthonous body, several alternatives were conceived . . . The simplest one, if we think of North America and Australia, was of course to move or remove the other body. Another one is to pretend that space is being divided and allocated to separate bodies. South Africa's rulers cling to that solution. Most often the preferred strategy has been simply to manipulate the other variable—Time. With the help of various devices of sequencing and distancing, one assigns to the conquered populations a different Time. A good deal of such Aristotelian political physics is reflected in the schemes of evolutionists and their cousins, the diffusionists.[35]

While Victorian evolutionary anthropology claimed to draw its conclusions only from objective data and apolitical scientific reasoning, the temporal trajectories it described were "anything but historically or politically neutral."[36]

Strikingly, White deploys the language of temporal distancing almost immediately before he advocates the permanent spatial separation of deviant and diseased bodies from "a healthy people."[37] The proximate use of

32. Fabian, *Time and the Other*, 31.
33. Fabian, *Time and the Other*, 29.
34. Fabian, *Time and the Other*, 29.
35. Fabian, *Time and the Other*, 30.
36. Fabian, *Time and the Other*, 17.
37. White, *Efficiency and Empire*, 120.

these two forms of distancing in the text may be related to the difficulty of segregating fit and unfit Anglo-Saxons from each other, instead of colonized people marked as different by race. In a context where charitable care for the poor and sick was assumed to be a religious and moral duty, those to be segregated physically would first need to be differentiated from the community rhetorically. White's solution to the traditional English concepts of liberty and Christian charity, then, is to strip the unfit of the protections of English identity.[38]

We Are Still "Coming Apart"

Compared with *Efficiency and Empire*, twenty-first-century texts on American decline and renewal are generally more subtle and indirect in their support of eugenics. One of the much less subtle writers on this subject is Charles Murray, author of a notorious text on race and intelligence (*The Bell Curve*), as well the much more recent *Coming Apart: The State of White America, 1960–2010*. In the latter, he warns that working-class white Americans are increasingly living in contexts that resemble African-American communities, and less like those of middle- and upper-class white communities. From virtues such as industriousness, honesty, and religiosity, to the rates of marriage and unwed pregnancy, Murray finds contemporary poor white Americans lacking in the virtues and behaviors that united an earlier generation of white people across the social classes. Instead, he argues that their actions and attitudes have increasingly come to resemble those of African-Americans. In short, poor white people are in danger of losing their whiteness.

Describing this "new lower class," he writes that "individually, they're not much of a problem," but "collectively, they can destroy the kind of civil society that America requires."[39] Ultimately, he traces this threat to what he sees as the pathologies of the welfare state, especially in replacing the heterosexual nuclear family and the church as institutions of social support. In some ways, Murray's proposals are the libertarian mirror image of White's coercive eugenic policies. While White was concerned with prohibiting

38. This pattern would repeat itself even more tragically in 1930s Germany, where one of the first steps of the Holocaust involved evicting German Jews from the category of "Germanness" and redefining them as a dangerous biopolitical threat to the life and health of the social body.

39. Murray, *Coming Apart*, 209.

marriages between unhealthy or underaged citizens, Murray focuses on encouraging marriage as a means to social and economic stability. In both cases, the control of marriage and reproduction, and thus of the population, is at stake, even though the role of direct coercion has changed. Murray's version of soft eugenics deploys research in neuroscience and genetics to explain why social structures are the way they are, why they will never change, and therefore why the US should dismantle its welfare state:

> Harvard's Edward O. Wilson anticipated what is to come in a book titled *Consilience*. As the twenty-first century progresses, he argued, the social sciences are increasingly going to be shaped by the findings of biology—specifically, the findings of the neuroscientists and the geneticists.
>
> I am predicting that over the next few decades advances in evolutionary psychology are going to be conjoined with advances in genetic understanding, leading to a scientific consensus that goes something like this: There are genetic reasons, rooted in the mechanisms of human evolution, why little boys who grow up in neighborhoods without married fathers tend to reach adolescence not socialized to the norms of behavior that they will need to stay out of prison and to hold jobs. These same reasons explain why child abuse is, and always will be, concentrated among family structures in which the live-in male is not the married biological father. These same reasons explain why society's attempts to compensate for the lack of married biological fathers don't work and will never work.[40]

Murray's citation of biologist E. O. Wilson here is telling, and Wilson will play a key role in the next chapter. For now, it is important to note how Murray uses the language of genetics to make a purely political argument based on scientific knowledge that does not currently exist, but which he hopes will exist one day.[41]

---

40. Murray, *Coming Apart*, 299.

41. The field of epigenetics, which among other things researches the effects of environment on inherited traits, is one of the most contested disciplines in the biological sciences. Recent widely publicized research has suggested, for example, that the experiences of Holocaust survivors caused genetic changes in their descendants. See Yehuda et al., "Holocaust Exposure Induced Intergenerational Effects," 372–80. However, this paper has also been criticized for its small sample size and inconclusive results. See Birney, "Why I'm Skeptical About the Idea of Genetically Inherited Trauma." Given that the history of science is replete with examples of misattributing politically convenient phenomena to genetics, caution is in order.

Here, as throughout the text, Murray uses temporal distancing to conflate American poverty with cultural savagery, especially among the boys and young men he variously describes as "not socialized" (and thus uncivilized), violent, and indolent. In fact, he argues the only way these young men can join the temporal present is through marriage:

> George Gilder was mostly right [when he wrote] that unmarried males arriving at adulthood are barbarians who are then civilized by women through marriage. The inflammatory part was that Gilder saw disaster looming as women stopped performing this function, a position derided as the worst kind of patriarchal sexism. But, put in less vivid language, the argument is neither implausible nor inflammatory. The responsibilities of marriage induce young men to settle down, focus, and get to work.[42]

Now, as in the nineteenth century, it is the role of women to save men, and thereby to save the well-being of the nation, by civilizing them into domesticity, productivity, and citizenship.

Against All Enemies, Foreign and Domestic

Murray's appeal to the stereotypical civilizing role of married women is intriguing, especially in a book that ends in full-throated praise of the American project as "a different way for people to live together, unique among the nations of the earth, and immeasurably precious."[43] This intersection of domestic felicity and American exceptionalism can helpfully be unpacked through a reading of Amy Kaplan's essay "Manifest Domesticity," in which she argues the concept of the domestic is most fruitfully held in tension not to the concept of the public, or to what is often called civil society, but to that of the foreign. Moreover, she suggests the notion of the foreign as the stage upon which the politics of grand strategy are enacted is dependent on, and produced by, the concept of the domestic. Domesticity is not a "separate sphere" from what is often understood as the arena of politics. As Kaplan explains,

> This deconstruction of separate spheres . . . leaves another structural opposition intact: the domestic in intimate opposition to the foreign. In this context domestic has a double meaning that

42. Murray, *Coming Apart*, 181–82.
43. Murray, *Coming Apart*, 306.

not only links the familial household to the nation but also imag-
ines both in opposition to everything outside the geographic and
conceptual border of the home. The earliest meaning of foreign,
according to the *OED*, is "out of doors" or "at a distance from
home." Contemporary English speakers refer to national concerns
as domestic in explicit or implicit contrast with the foreign. The
notion of domestic policy makes sense only in opposition to foreign policy, and uncoupled from the foreign, national issues are
never labeled domestic. The idea of foreign policy depends on the
sense of the nation as a domestic space imbued with a sense of
at-homeness, in contrast to an external world perceived as alien
and threatening. Reciprocally, a sense of the foreign is necessary to
erect the boundaries that enclose the nation as a home.[44]

Specifically, travel into the geographical spaces marked as foreign depends
on a sense of the domestic. A well-ordered home and a well-ordered geography of exploration, scientific discovery, and colonial expansion depend
upon each other, and, indeed, are produced by each other. As Kaplan
writes, "through the process of domestication, the home contains within
itself those wild or foreign elements that must be tamed: domesticity not
only monitors the borders between the civilized and the savage but also
regulates traces of the savage within itself."[45]

It can be tempting to assume the discipline of political theology is
only concerned with events on the large scale, whether the global arena
of the machinations of nation-states or the common life of cities. But it
is a mistake to draw a boundary around the home as an apolitical zone
that does not also participate in the interactions between the political, the
soteriological, and the temporal. At first glance, Murray's work seems to be
focused on matters of domestic policy, in both senses of the word. However, as Kaplan insists, "the notion of domestic policy makes sense only in
opposition to foreign policy, and uncoupled from the foreign, national issues are never labeled domestic."[46] Murray's deviant American and White's
epileptic Englishman can only be temporally marked as domestic barbar-
ians because the figure of the foreign barbarian exists. It is to this question
of the relationship between the constitution of human beings as modern
subjects in domestic and foreign spaces that this chapter now turns.

44. Kaplan, "Manifest Domesticity," 581–82.

45. Kaplan, "Manifest Domesticity," 581.

46. Kaplan, "Manifest Domesticity," 581.

Fear of Falling

How, and in what ways, did the logic of colonialism produce the modern self within the borders of European nation-states? How is the distinction between properly constituted and deviant identity brought to bear on Europeans and white Americans to separate them into categories? As Ann Laura Stoler explains in *Race and the Education of Desire*, the role played by colonialism in the production of European identity has long been underestimated, even as in colonial settings "Europeans imagined themselves in the colonies and cultivated their distinctions from those to be ruled."[47]

This process of differentiation begins in the encounter with indigenous people who were to be turned into colonial subjects. Stoler writes that a "century of racial discourse" had already been "loaded with a barrage of colonial representations of savagery, licentiousness, and other basic truths about human nature."[48] These representations would expand across both European and colonial geographies, tying the "'others' of empire" to "the 'other' within Europe itself."[49] The bourgeois European subject, and his middle-class sensibilities, would be constituted through a process of differentiation from his racial and economic inferiors:

> Colonialism was not a secure bourgeois project. It was not only about the importation of middle-class sensibilities to the colonies but about the making of them. This is not to suggest that middle-class European prescriptions were invented out of whole cloth in the outposts of empire and only then brought back home. [T]he philanthropic moralizing mission that defined bourgeois culture in the nineteenth century cast a wide imperial net . . . the distinctions defining bourgeois sexuality were played out against not only the bodies of an immoral European working class and native other, but against those of destitute whites in the colonies and in dubious contrast to an ambiguous population of mixed-blood origin. If we accept that 'whiteness' was part of the moral re-armament of bourgeois society, then we need to investigate that contingent relationship between European racial and class anxieties in the colonies and bourgeois cultivations of self in England, Holland, and France.[50]

47. Stoler, *Race and the Education of Desire*, 98.
48. Stoler, *Race and the Education of Desire*, 128.
49. Stoler, *Race and the Education of Desire*, 128.
50. Stoler, *Race and the Education of Desire*, 100.

Although the concept of "whiteness," or properly constituted European identity, was important to this process of renewal, it was far from a stable category. According to Stoler, there was an ongoing "subterranean colonial discourse" that "anxiously debated who was truly European," and "whether those who were both poor and white should be included among them."[51] Whiteness, or European identity, was therefore understood as an impermanent state that could be lost.

The figure of the bourgeois subject was, as Eric Hobsbawm writes, "if not a different species," then at least "the member of a superior race, a higher stage in human evolution, distinct from the lower orders who remained in the historical or cultural equivalent of childhood or adolescence."[52] By comparison, the white working class occupied an earlier temporal location and a primitive identity, distanced from the historical present by their lack of self-control, and in particular by their promiscuity. As Sharon Tiffany and Kathleen Adams note, the figure of the working-class woman in Victorian England was marked precisely in this way as a "primitive relic of an earlier evolutionary period," as a "wild woman" whose potential to unleash sexual chaos in urban industrial areas was set over against the "moral model" of "middle-class sexual restraint and civility."[53]

Stoler's account of the complex and transient nature of European identity in the colonial period is also helpful for reading Charles Murray's work on what he calls contemporary "white America." Writing in the conclusion of *Coming Apart*, Murray alludes to a passage in Arnold J. Toynbee's controversial *A Study of History* that describes an ostensibly universal pattern of civilizational decline:

> Toynbee took up the processes that lead to the disintegration of civilizations. His argument went like this: The growth phase of a civilization is led by a creative minority with a strong, self-confident sense of style, virtue, and purpose. The uncreative majority follows along. Then, at some point in every civilization's journey, the creative minority degenerates into a dominant minority, its members still run the show, but they are no longer confident and no longer set the example. Among other reactions are a "lapse into truancy"—a rejection of the obligations of citizenship—and "surrender to a sense of promiscuity"—vulgarization of manners,

51. Stoler, *Race and the Education of Desire*, 103.

52. Cited in Stoler, *Race and the Education of Desire*, 126.

53. Tiffany and Adams, cited in Stoler, "Cultivating Bourgeois Bodies and Racial Selves," 107.

the arts, and language—that "are apt to appear first in the ranks of the proletariat and to spread from there to the ranks of the dominant minority, which usually succumbs to the sickness of 'proletarianization.'"[54]

Murray describes the "shock of recognition" he experienced on reading this passage, tying it to the "adoption by the middle class and upper-middle-class of behaviors that used to be distinctly lower-class" in the contemporary United States.[55] He lists four examples of this societal slide towards primitivism, most notably the popularity of "the hooker look" among "nice girls from the suburbs."[56] This, he continues, "is what happens when civilizations are headed downhill."[57]

In rejecting the model of sexual restraint crucial to the formation of middle-class domesticity, these dangerous women threaten to drag the nation down the temporal slope with them into primitivity. No longer easily distinguishable from each other, the images of the promiscuous "wild woman" and the "nice girl," the dangerous working-class woman and the icon of middle-class virtue, converge into one.[58] In Arnold White's industrial England, just as in Charles Murray's America, the problem of unstable European identity is described as a problem of moral declension, where the "collapse of a sturdy elite code"[59] of behavior has prevented the upper class from setting the proper moral tone for the childlike lower classes to emulate.[60]

Let the reader understand that I am emphatically not in favor of promiscuity, or fornication, or the inappropriate marketing of suggestive fashions to young girls. As St. Paul might say, "By no means!" Here I am concerned with the political deployments that name sex and childbirth outside of marriage as a particular and even unique pathology of poor and working-class people, and as a temporal danger to the nation. What marks some homes as bastions of domesticity and others as the sites where the primitive state of nature threatens to erupt from within the social body and

54. Murray, *Coming Apart*, 286.

55. Murray, *Coming Apart*, 286.

56. Murray, *Coming Apart*, 286.

57. Murray, *Coming Apart*, 287.

58. Murray, *Coming Apart*, 128.

59. Murray, *Coming Apart*, 289.

60. As I noted in chapter 2, the specter of sexual chaos in urban industrial areas also played a key role in the formation of the Social Gospel movement.

destroy it? More to the theological point, how is the latter placed outside the category of the neighbor?

Christianity without Christ

Most books on national decline and renewal include a discussion of "religion" as a category of social activity and source of moral norms, and the examples discussed in this chapter are no exception. Murray's notion of "religiosity" is based on the moral and social benefits of church attendance. The content of belief in these texts is, in itself, unimportant. For Arnold White, the role of the Church of England was similar: "to create and maintain, throughout all ranks, a high standard of decent and moral existence."[61] As he explains, "So far as an Established Church increases morality, and raises the standard of public conduct, it is an instrument of efficiency."[62] Finally, Peter Kiernan states his opposition to "religious fervor" and "religious activists" of all sorts, including the opponents of stem cell research he derides as "embryo defenders."[63] Instead, he calls for "compromise" and moderation, explaining that "we lose sight of everything if we let one dogma or another completely define us. The notions of fairness and balance can be found in texts and holy writ of every religion."[64] The role of "radical centrists" like himself, then, is "to lead everyone back to every religion's first premise—Love one another."[65]

In each case, the particularity of Christian doctrine and Christian Scripture has been eliminated, and what remains is merely a series of decontextualized moral precepts closer to the words of Benjamin Franklin than those of Jesus Christ. What is "religion" as a category in these accounts, and what work does its deployment do? What does the commandment to love one another mean without either a particular God who commands or an account of love? This is civil religion at its finest, deployed in the service of the state instead of God. And, as Samuel P. Huntington once described with approval, this civil religion of the United States may have some things in common with Christianity, but it is emphatically *not* itself Christian:

---

61. White, *Efficiency and Empire*, 88.
62. White, *Efficiency and Empire*, 88.
63. Kiernan, *Becoming China's Bitch*, 106.
64. Kiernan, *Becoming China's Bitch*, 106.
65. Kiernan, *Becoming China's Bitch*, 107.

America's civil religion is a nondenominational, national religion and, in its articulated form, not expressly a Christian religion. Yet it is thoroughly Christian in its origin, content, assumptions, and tone. The God in whom their currency says Americans trust is implicitly the Christian God. Two words, nonetheless, do not appear in civil religion statements and ceremonies. They are "Jesus Christ." While the American Creed is Protestantism without God, the American civil religion is Christianity without Christ.[66]

The problem with these forms of civil religion is not only that they represent a deformation of Christianity. The problem is they tempt Christians to accept such a deformation in the name of making the faith relevant to civic discourse and societal improvement. But in doing so, it is far too easy to sell the inheritance of Esau for a meal ticket that in the end fails to sustain.

Duty's "Shall"

The theological politics of our existence in time are not only a matter of dislocating ourselves or our neighbors in time or in space. They are also a matter of looking to the wrong agent of salvation to give us our time, and ourselves, back again. We turn once again to Kierkegaard, and in particular to his unmasking of the problems that lurk within the image of domestic bliss put forward in *Either/Or II*, where Judge William gives his account of "The Esthetic Validity of Marriage." There, the self-satisfied middle-class husband describes himself as having produced his own salvation and grounded his own existence in time through his "struggles with time"—struggles in which he emerges victorious through his consuming grasp of the domestic tranquility ensured by his wife.[67] As Judge William puts it, only through marriage can one find the unity between time and eternity and the resolution of recollection and hope:

> [The married man] has not fought with lions and trolls but with the most dangerous enemy, which is time. But now eternity does not come forward, as for the knight, but he has eternity in time, has preserved eternity in time. Therefore only he has been victorious over time, for it may be said of the knight that he has killed time, just as one to whom time has no reality always wishes to kill time, but this is never the right victory. Like a true victor, the

66. Huntington, *Who Are We?*, 106.
67. Kierkegaard, *Either/Or II*, 134.

married man has not killed time but has rescued and preserved it in all eternity.[68]

Marital love, which he describes as the only form of "true love," has "an utterly different value." It "does its work in time" and in fact has "a completely different idea of time and of repetition."[69]

The judge's married life is for him the means of his salvation, and his God is conveniently reduced to "an eyewitness who does not cramp one's style."[70] In particular, he looks to his wife as the mediator who grounds his existence in time, giving it meaning and coherence:

> If, when I am sitting in my study and time is dragging for me, I slip into the living room, I sit down in a corner, I say not a word for fear of disturbing her in her task, for even though it looks like a game, it is done with a dignity and decorum that inspires respect, and she is far from being what you say Mrs. Hansen is, a top that hums and buzzes around and by its humming and buzzing makes matrimonial music in the living room.[71]

For Judge William, then, "the woman" is the key to the existence of "the man" in time. As he explains with an almost ecstatic fervor,

> Is it a perfection in a woman, this secret rapport she has with time; is it an imperfection? Is it because she has a more earthly creature than the man, or because she has more eternity within her? Please do answer; after all, you have a philosophic mind. When I am sitting this way, desolate and lost, and then I watch my wife moving lightly and youthfully around the room, always busy—she always has something to take care of—my eyes involuntarily follow her movements. I participate in everything she is doing, and in the end I find myself within time again, time has meaning for me again, and the moment hurries along again.[72]

Heretically, Judge William also contends that married life has brought him to a state of self-knowledge, such that "through the individual's intercourse with himself the individual is made pregnant by himself and gives birth to

---

68. Kierkegaard, *Either/Or II*, 138.

69. Kierkegaard, *Either/Or II*, 141.

70. Kierkegaard, *Either/Or II*, 56.

71. Kierkegaard, *Either/Or II*, 308.

72. Kierkegaard, *Either/Or II*, 307.

himself."[73] In marriage, Judge William escapes the paradox of time in and through himself, but by means of an assimilative and acquisitive consumption of his wife as the salvific "woman." As what may at first seem to be a detour through *Either/Or* reminds us, colonizing voyages of discovery may not save, but neither does what happens within the contours of self-satisfied married life. The problem of misplaced salvation on the global political stage cannot be solved by turning within the boundaries of the home.

You Shall Love

While Kierkegaard can tell us much about looking to the wrong place and the wrong people to ground our existence in time, he can also reorient us in the right direction. Writing in *Philosophical Fragments*, he playfully turns and returns to the question of time and of contemporaneity with Christ and, in turn, with the neighbors we are given to see and love through Christ. In *Philosophical Fragments*, Kierkegaard contrasts Christian existence with what he calls "the Socratic," wherein truth lies within the individual and may be extracted through a process of self-knowledge. Again and again, he returns to the refrain "if the moment is to have decisive significance," arguing that such a moment is not Socratically self-generated but received as sheer, gratuitous gift.[74]

This moment, which occasions the unity between God and humanity, time and eternity, teacher and learner, occurs not by means of a human ascent (even a divinely assisted ascent) to a pinnacle of exaltation. Rather, it takes place "by means of a descent," in which God takes on "the form of a servant," not just as a divine means of disguise and concealment, but truly and completely. As he writes,

> For this is the boundlessness of love, that in earnestness and truth and not in jest it wills to be the equal of the beloved, and it is the omnipotence of resolving love to be capable of that of which neither the king nor Socrates was capable, which is why their assumed characters were still a kind of deceit.[75]

As he continues, Kierkegaard shows Judge William's tactic of do-it-yourself salvation and maritally grounded temporality for the lie that it is:

73. Kierkegaard, *Either/Or II*, 259.
74. Kierkegaard, *Philosophical Fragments*, 28.
75. Kierkegaard, *Philosophical Fragments*, 32.

The god's love—if he wants to be a teacher—must not only be an assisting love but a procreative love by which he gives birth to the learner, or, as we have called him, one born again, meaning the transition from "not to be" to "to be." The truth, then, is that the learner owes him everything. But that which makes understanding so difficult is precisely this: that he becomes nothing and yet is not annihilated; that he owes him everything and yet becomes boldly confident; that he understands the truth, but the truth makes him free; that he grasps the guilt of untruth, and then again bold confidence triumphs in the truth. Between one human being and another, to be of assistance is supreme, but to beget is reserved for the god, whose love is procreative, but not that procreative love of which Socrates knew how to speak so beautifully on a festive occasion.[76]

To exist in time, in that decisive moment, is to simultaneously exist in debt to the one who has given us everything, and also with the neighbor whom that one commands us with duty's imperative: "You shall love."[77]

While some theological accounts of Christian love, such as that of Thomas Aquinas, proceed from a generally defined and understood account of love, Søren Kierkegaard's *Works of Love* proceeds from the opposite direction. Several crucial, but easily overlooked, framing devices at the beginning of *Works of Love* hint at Kierkegaard's intent. The first is the subtitle, "Christian deliberations in the form of discourses." This description distinguishes *Works of Love* from the "upbuilding discourses" that were also published under Kierkegaard's own name. A discourse on love assumes the reader knows what love is and tries to win her to it. A deliberation, on the other hand, attempts to dialectically overturn the reader's comfortable ways of thinking. *Works of Love* is intended as this latter, dialectic, form, as a disturbance of any easy assumption on the part of the reader that they already know what love is. Near the beginning of the first series of *Works of Love*, Kierkegaard parses the commandment "You shall love the neighbor" by unpacking the implications of each word except for "love" (*you* shall love the neighbor, you *shall* love the neighbor, you shall love *the neighbor*).

Drawing a sharp contrast between Christian love and *eros*, Kierkegaard maintains that the former is only understood as a divinely commanded duty ("you shall"), and not as a love of preference. Furthermore, he argues that love of the neighbor must be mediated by God in Christ, who stands as

---

76. Kierkegaard, *Philosophical Fragments*, 31.
77. Kierkegaard, *Works of Love*, 24.

the "middle term" between the lover and the beloved. Without this middle term, all human attempts to love ultimately collapse into a grasping and consuming form of self-love. Here, the beloved is eclipsed by the projection of another self, the "other I."[78]

One of the most striking features of Kierkegaard's account of love is his emphatic rejection of preferential love. Loves of preference, whether based on kinship or proximity, are antithetical to love of the neighbor. The neighbor is the one who is our equal before God, and every person (including the enemy) has this equality "unconditionally."[79] Importantly for the purposes of this chapter, the neighbor cannot only be those with whom I share preferences or culture. Rather, she is " one who is equal," not "the beloved, for whom you have passion's preference," or "your friend, for whom you have passion's preference," or "if you are a cultured person, the cultured individual with whom you have a similarity of culture—since with your neighbor you have the equality of a human being before God."[80] Love of the neighbor, Kierkegaard writes, "is equality."[81]

This meditation on the neighbor may usefully be read alongside chapter IIIA, "Romans 13:10. Love Is the Fulfilling of the Law," to bring the latent christological themes in *Works of Love* to the foreground. Christ, as Love, is "the fulfilling of the Law," and in and through him the world has received "the divine explanation of what love is."[82] Christ is both the *explainer* and the *explanation* of what love is:

> Christ was the fulfilling of the Law. How this thought is to be understood we are to learn from him, because he was the explanation, and only when the explanation is what it explains, when the explainer is what is explained, when the explanation is the transfiguration, only then is the relation the right one. Alas, we are unable to explain in this way.[83]

This text reveals the logic of using the Christian deliberation as a genre, and thus not assuming the definition of love in advance:

---

78. Kierkegaard, *Works of Love*, 57.
79. Kierkegaard, *Works of Love*, 60.
80. Kierkegaard, *Works of Love*, 60.
81. Kierkegaard, *Works of Love*, 60.
82. Kierkegaard, *Works of Love*, 110, 121.
83. Kierkegaard, *Works of Love*, 121.

If anyone asks, "What is love," Paul answers, "It is the fulfilling of the Law," and instantly every further question is precluded by that answer . . . Frequently in this world the question "what is love?" has certainly been asked out of curiosity, and frequently there has been some idler who in answering became involved with the curious asker, and these two, curiosity and idleness, liked each other so much that they were almost incapable of becoming tired of each other or of asking and answering the question.[84]

The answer to the question of love, from both Paul and Jesus, "imprisons" the one asking the question in "obedience under the Law." The Law was and is "everyone's downfall," because no one could fulfill its requirements; Christ was what the Law required, and he became the "downfall of the Law."[85]

The entirety of Jesus' life, as the fulfillment of the Law, was "a horrible collision with the merely human conception of what love is."[86] This "collision" can recur if we try to sequester the loves of preference, such as erotic love or friendship, from the stringency of the divine requirement and the totality of our need for God's intervention:

Love is a passion of the emotions, but in this emotion a person, even before he relates to the object of love, should first relate to God and thereby learn the requirement, that love is the fulfilling of the Law. . . . The love that does not lead to God, the love that does not have the single goal of leading the lovers to love God, stops with the merely human judgment of what love is and what love's sacrifice and giving of itself are; it stops and thereby avoids the possibility of the horror of the final and most terrible collision: that in the love-relationship there is the difference of infinity between the conceptions of what love is.[87]

Throughout the text, Kierkegaard tries to use what he calls the "school-yoke of the commandment" to thrust the reader back on her need for grace in all her works of love. Christ stands as the middle term in every relationship, even the most intimate, as every relationship stands in need of mercy and grace. At the same time, Kierkegaard is just as relentlessly clear on the identity of the neighbor to be loved. As Christ is our contemporary, the middle

84. Kierkegaard, *Works of Love*, 95–96.
85. Kierkegaard, *Works of Love*, 96.
86. Kierkegaard, *Works of Love*, 96.
87. Kierkegaard, *Works of Love*, 96.

term in all our fumbling attempts to love, he has made us contemporaries of each other as well. There is no room for the tactics of temporal distancing and the denial of coevalness in the love commanded of disciples. And so, this distancing in time is not only a problem of thought or scholarship, but also of the politics of daily life on the most mundane of levels.

Love and Praise

In paragraph 18 of Volume I/2 of the *Church Dogmatics* ("The Life of the Children of God"), Karl Barth gives his own account of Christian love, its object, and its effects. He begins not from a definition of love as such, but from a short account of the "Christian *in concreto*," the concretely existing recipient of the revelation of the word.[88] This is the "free man" who has been "claimed" as a "specific subject and being," and "newly made in the relationship created between himself and God." This "new subject" is not subsistent as being, but only in the "specific doing" of "seeking after God" in the sense of Colossians 3:1. His inward being-in-doing is "the love of God in the transitive sense"—the "love of man to God."[89] The corresponding outward act is the "praise of God" that is "inescapably laid upon us when our freedom is transferred to another action under the sentence and judgment of God when we are dead with Christ."[90] The Christian life, therefore, is the "life of the children of God" comprised of "love and praise."[91] Barth argues that, as a human response to the love of God for humanity, Christian love "must correspond on man's side to that which is said by God on His side." But a faithful definition of "love" is difficult to produce, since "we all think we know already about human loving," and "we continue to do so even when confronted by the fact of the love of God to us."[92] Clearly, this is an account of love that is vastly different from the nebulous and politically malleable version espoused by Peter Kiernan.

Human beings tend to "forget" the discipline of Scripture, or attempt to evade it "in favor of some preconceived idea of love in general." But Barth reminds us that if we do so, our definition of Christian love may be derived "from a false source." As a "relative guarantee" against this possibility, Barth

88. Barth, *Church Dogmatics* I/2, 366.
89. Barth, *Church Dogmatics* I/2, 369–70.
90. Barth, *Church Dogmatics* I/2, 371.
91. Barth, *Church Dogmatics* I/2, 371.
92. Barth, *Church Dogmatics* I/2, 380.

turns to a close reading of Scripture. His approach here to the summary of the Law in Mark is similar to his previous exegesis of John 1:14 as a focal text for the doctrine of the incarnation.[93] In one particularly compelling passage, Barth's commentary on "the Lord our God is one Lord" inverts the logic of lordship, rule, and mastery to proclaim the Master who took the form of a servant:

> As their Master he does not belong to a genus, in which there are others who can also rule over them. Apart from His, there may be all sorts of other so-called, supposed and apparent spheres and therefore all sorts of other so-called, supposed and apparent lords. But no one else rules and is the Lord as He is, i.e., in deed and in truth . . . He gives himself to be the bearer of their shame and curse; He suffers in their place, that they may be acquitted and free. For that reason His control is a unique control. It is a control which at first sight is quite definitely not what we mean by ruling and commanding. It is not a matter of demands and claims and orders. On the contrary, it is all gift and offer and promise.[94]

This gift entails the absolute commandment to love, but it is a commandment like no other. Barth uses Kierkegaard's *Works of Love* (the topic of the final section) to describe the commandment to love as a "happy obligation" that "in its divinity is a means of blessing."[95] While it does not "have its origin in our hearts," neither is it "an alien demand that comes to us from without." Instead, it is "the demand to be what we are" as the children of God.[96] The love of God "takes place in the self-knowledge of repentance," whereby we "learn about ourselves by the mirror of the Word of God" that "acquits and blesses us."[97] And, even as our own being and activity stands under judgment, that being and activity is given a *telos*, "at the point where everything is done for us," in "the direction Godward in Jesus Christ."[98]

93. Barth, *Church Dogmatics* I/2, 381.
94. Barth, *Church Dogmatics* I/2, 383.
95. Barth, *Church Dogmatics* I/2, 386.
96. Barth, *Church Dogmatics* I/2, 386.
97. Barth, *Church Dogmatics* I/2, 390.
98. Barth, *Church Dogmatics* I/2, 392.

Love of God and Love of Neighbor

How are the love of God and the love of the neighbor related? Barth takes a typically creative approach to the relationship between the two commandments. In his reading of the text, there are three common (but unsatisfactory) interpretations of the scriptural language of "first" and "second" commandments. The first reading is "there are two absolute commandments side by side," implying everything commanded in regard to the love of God also applies to the love of the neighbor and thus opening the door to "the love of two Gods."[99] The second is to "regard the two loves as identical," and thus to "interpret love to God as love to the neighbor and love to the neighbor as love to God." But Barth rejects this as well, on the basis of the "illegitimate" assumptions it makes in the domain of theological anthropology.[100] He states,

> It is inevitable that the distinctive features of a love to God which cannot be seen should be known and therefore necessarily determined by a love to man which is very much seen and supposedly well known. Love to God is, then, the quintessence and hypostasized expression of what we know in a concretely perceptible and practical form as love to man. Love to God is the idea, the supreme norm of this known love to man.[101]

Here, the problem for Barth is that the "converse" notion—that true love of the neighbor "must also be love to God"—is one that "comes too late to be a real converse."[102] The result of this imbalance is a form of liberal Protestant humanism in which "there is no praise of the God who has first loved us, breaking forth in love to the neighbor. Instead, there is praise of the sanctity and dignity and glory of man, with a somewhat equivocal love for the God created according to the likeness of this man."[103]

The third possible interpretation of the commandment is to "separate the commandment to love the neighbor from the absolute commandment to love God, and to regard it as one of the relative, derived, and subordinate commandments, as a summary of the commandments of the second table, and yet as such only a repetition and commentary on the first

---

99. Barth, *Church Dogmatics* I/2, 402.
100. Barth, *Church Dogmatics* I/2, 403.
101. Barth, *Church Dogmatics* I/2, 403.
102. Barth, *Church Dogmatics* I/2, 403.
103. Barth, *Church Dogmatics* I/2, 403.

commandment, the commandment to love God."[104] The difficulty here is that the commandment of God is "always" an "absolute commandment," and thus there can be no sense of primary and subordinate requirements that lessens the stringency of the requirement to love the neighbor.[105]

As a solution, Barth suggests a "way which is different from the first and" which "cannot be substituted for or confused with it," but which still maintains the force of the commandment itself. This solution takes into account the temporal location of the church, "in the space between the resurrection and the ascension watching and waiting . . . in two times and two worlds."[106] This eschatological approach allows Barth to draw out some of the "elements of truth" from each of the three previously rejected proposals. The commandment to love God is "intended for the child of God in his completed existence in Jesus Christ as the heavenly Head of his earthly members," while the commandment to love the neighbor is "intended for the child of God in his not yet completed walk and activity as an earthly member of the heavenly Head." These commandments cannot be merged into each other, even as they both "have to do with the one claim of the one God" on each human being. In addition, they are "not symmetrical" insofar as "love to God is the real cause and expository principle of love to the neighbor" and "love to the neighbor is in fact the token of love to God," the "erecting of a sign, and not of a completed and eternal work."[107] The commandment to love the neighbor is "enclosed" by and "contained" within the commandment to love God, and "to that extent" is "inferior" to it. But at the same time, and "for that very reason," it also "shares its absoluteness."[108] The love of the neighbor is a "sign," to be sure, but it is a sign "which is demanded from us" absolutely.[109]

As Barth explains, the definition of the neighbor requires further explication. The commandment to love the neighbor operates on a different logic than relationships arising from the existing orders of natural and political affinity:

> [W]e shall have to treat with some reserve the advice frequently
> given by Luther, that we must seek out neighbor within the orders

104. Barth, *Church Dogmatics* I/2, 406.
105. Barth, *Church Dogmatics* I/2, 407.
106. Barth, *Church Dogmatics* I/2, 411.
107. Barth, *Church Dogmatics* I/2, 411.
108. Barth, *Church Dogmatics* I/2, 411.
109. Barth, *Church Dogmatics* I/2, 411.

of life and society in which we actually find ourselves: the husband in the wife, the children in their parents and brothers and sisters, the master in the servant, the inferior in the superiors and vice versa, the national in the fellow-national and so on. . . . The neighbor cannot . . . be thought of as a kind of content of the mandate, claimed by human society, in all its various forms. The mandate does, of course, exist, but it owes its dignity and validity to a form of the neighbor in which he does not face us as a representative of the mandate, or as an authority to which we owe obedience and service.[110]

The neighbor to whom Christian love is due confronts us in another form, as the one who reveals the "plight of man" in his affliction, and who bears "an actual similarity to the crucified Jesus Christ."[111] The neighbor is the afflicted one who "shows me that I myself am a sinner"[112]:

> Only afflicted, sinful man can [summon us to the praise of God]. Only this man is my neighbor in the sense of the second commandment. But this neighbor will give me a really mortal headache. . . . The wretched fellow-man beside me simply reveals to me in his existence my own misery. . . . This is the criterion: if it is otherwise, if I can still see him without seeing myself, then for all the direct sympathy I may have for him, for all the zeal and sacrifice I may perhaps offer him, I have not really seen him.[113]

The encounter with the neighbor, then, is the encounter with one who "holds up a mirror" into which we "would rather not look," and in whose reflection we are shown ourselves in all our own sin and affliction.[114]

The rhetorical tactics of temporal distancing and of the denial of coevalness described in this chapter are not only an unfortunate artifact of scientific hubris, or limited to the histories of colonial domination. Rather, they are a symptom of a profound political and moral distortion, rooted in the past but all too pervasive in the present. While a reading of Kierkegaard and Barth provides a sharp word otherwise to those who would distance themselves in time from their neighbors, its political implications extend far beyond the anthropological or the philosophical realms. The problem

110. Barth, *Church Dogmatics* I/2, 416.
111. Barth, *Church Dogmatics* I/2, 429, 431.
112. Barth, *Church Dogmatics* I/2, 431.
113. Barth, *Church Dogmatics* I/2, 431.
114. Barth, *Church Dogmatics* I/2, 432.

that these thinkers diagnose is not only a problem of thought or scholar-ship, but also of political speech on the most mundane of levels. Indeed, the aforementioned temporal maneuvers can also be found in the popular rhetoric that surrounds political debate, especially insofar as that rhetoric emerges from within Western liberalism itself.

Rather than argue against a policy on its merits (or on the lack there-of), many political activists focus instead on the perceived temporal rever-sion it represents, painting it as a step backwards into the past and away from contemporaneity. In this form of liberal rhetoric, the *backwardness* of a political position in and of itself functions as self-evident proof of its *wrongness*. These habits of speech can be seen in debates on topics ranging from drug policy to energy regulation to religious freedom. One political position is posited as representing contemporaneity (or the future), while the other is cast as a retrograde attempt to pull the social body back down the temporal slope, and towards the position its proponents are assumed to occupy. And yet, as this chapter has suggested, such temporal distanc-ing makes political discernment and debate difficult, if not impossible to achieve. As a way to describe the contours of human life together, politi-cal conversation depends on the relationships that only contemporaneity makes possible. And that contemporaneity, in turn, depends on a recogni-tion that no human project is salvific. Thankfully, that job has already been taken by the one who places himself as the middle term between each of us and our neighbors even as he commands us to love them. As the Word made flesh, Jesus Christ has become our neighbor even as he becomes our Brother. The moment of the incarnation is also the moment in which hu-man relationships are grounded in the Christian life.

5

Beyond

At this point we leave Africa, not to mention it again. For it is no historical part of the World; it has no movement or development to exhibit.... What we properly understand by Africa, is the Unhistorical, Undeveloped Spirit, still involved in the conditions of mere nature, and which had to be presented here only as on the threshold of the World's History.

—G. W. F. HEGEL, *THE PHILOSOPHY OF HISTORY*[1]

Too bad that Hegel lacked time; but if one is to dispose of all of world history, how does one get time for the little test as to whether the absolute method, which explains everything, is also able to explain the life of a single human being? In ancient times, one would have smiled at a method that can explain all of world history absolutely but cannot explain a single person even mediocrely.

—SØREN KIERKEGAARD, REVISION OF PAP. V B 14[2]

Evolution means mutations and there are going to be losers who, 20,000 years ago, would not have lived very long. But now in our so-called compassionate society we should take care of them, but we do so very badly as they age. There are some born losers.

—JAMES WATSON[3]

1. Hegel, *Philosophy of History*, 99.
2. Kierkegaard, *Philosophical Fragments*, 206.
3. Lewis, "James Watson on 'Genetic Losers,'" para. 17.

But when the fullness of time had come, God sent his Son, born of a woman, born under the law, in order to redeem those who were under the law, so that we might receive adoption as children. And because you are children, God has sent the Spirit of his Son into our hearts, crying, "Abba! Father!" So you are no longer a slave but a child, and if a child then also an heir, through God.

—GALATIANS 4:4–7 (NRSV)

The first section of biologist E. O. Wilson's recent book, *The Meaning of Human Existence,* opens with a portentous epigraph printed in capital letters. Under the heading "The Reason We Exist," Wilson writes, "History makes little sense without prehistory, and prehistory makes little sense without biology. Knowledge of prehistory and biology is increasing rapidly, bringing into focus how humanity originated and why a species like our own exists on this planet."[4] Throughout his career as an authoritative popularizer of science, Wilson's argument has been consistent. In order to understand ourselves as human beings, we should view our own lives and the lives of others from an evolutionary perspective that encompasses all of time, from the origins of the universe to the present day. From that perspective, he argues, we can evaluate our own time as well as the past. We can determine for ourselves the form of the "fullness of time." In doing so, we can also determine, control, or manage the time of our neighbors as an undifferentiated totality.[5] Epistemology becomes politics. For Wilson, the biological question of how *homo sapiens* emerged as a species flows seamlessly into questions of anthropology and sociology.

Wilson is far from unique. Examples of this maneuver in evolutionary biology and anthropology can be seen in the work of contemporary popularizers of science like Jonathan Haidt and Jared Diamond. It also appears in the work of early evolutionary theorists like Ernst Haeckel, the German biologist who was an interlocutor for Barth in his doctrine of creation.[6] Lastly, it travels into theology, where it can create unintended moral and doctrinal consequences.

4. Wilson, *Meaning of Human Existence,* 10.

5. Recall that Wilson was approvingly cited by Charles Murray to buttress his argument against the welfare state.

6. See Haidt, *Righteous Mind,* and, "Why We Celebrate a Killing." See also Diamond, *Guns, Germs, and Steel; Collapse;* and *World Until Yesterday.*

One theological instance of this remote view-from-above can be found in the *Catechism of Creation*, written in 2005 by the Episcopal Church's Committee on Science, Technology, and Faith. Most of the *Catechism of Creation* is concerned with differentiating Episcopalians from the various permutations of what is generally called creationism in the American context. Its secondary purpose is to outline a theological basis for environmental stewardship. The constructive doctrine of creation it offers as an alternative to creationism relies on the idea that God creates "in, with, and under" evolutionary processes of natural selection.[7] To support their argument, they cite Charles Kingsley's words that "God has made a world that is able to make itself," yet without noting the nature of the world that Kingsley envisioned.[8]

For the authors of the *Catechism of Creation*, the view of time from an evolutionary perspective is an aid to the worship and contemplation of God. The authors write,

> The God of evolution is the biblical God, subtle and gracious, who interacts with and rejoices in the enormous variety, diversity, and beauty of this evolving creation. When we contemplate the tremendous gift of freedom God has bestowed upon the creation, and how the Holy Spirit preserves in covenantal faithfulness the physical laws, powers and processes that enable such variety and beauty, these thoughts may move our hearts to a deeper admiration, awe and gratitude for God's works. They may inspire a curiosity to know God's creation more deeply, celebrate it with thanksgiving, and devote ourselves to caring for it.[9]

From the sweeping perspective of evolutionary time, this may seem at first to be an attractive argument. If only the changes in populations and species over time are visible, then evolution appears be a positive process that ensures diversity and difference. It may even appear to be a process from which something may be inferred about God's activity in the world. But things look quite different on a human scale of time and place. What may look from afar like divine creativity looks instead like agonism, suffering, and death for the most vulnerable. Far from an indicator of divine activity,

7. The Episcopal Church in the United States of America, *Catechism of Creation*, 12.
8. The Episcopal Church in the United States of America, *Catechism of Creation*, 12.
9. The Episcopal Church in the United States of America, *Catechism of Creation*, 15.

it looks instead like a consequence of the fall from which no theological claims can be made.[10]

In this final chapter, I return in some sense to where I began, with questions of human origins and scientific authority. Here, I am concerned with the intellectual and political act in which the scientific authority, transparent to reason, places herself outside of time in order to evaluate the significance of the time, as well as to direct or control the time through the management of populations as an undifferentiated group. Then, I turn once more to Kierkegaard and Barth to question both the perspective from outside of time and the politics of scientific bureaucracy that emerge from that perspective and aspire to world-historical significance.

The View from Above

The Meaning of Human Existence: E. O. Wilson

E. O. Wilson rose to prominence writing on the biology of insects. But like many evolutionary biologists, from Darwin and Haeckel to the present day, his interests soon drifted towards the political and the philosophical. This intellectual trajectory began with the controversial *Sociobiology* (1975), continued with *Consilience* (1998), and has expanded in the past decade to include *The Social Conquest of Earth* (2012), the aforementioned *The Meaning of Human Existence* (2014), and *Genesis: The Deep Origin of Societies* (2019). A typical popular account of Wilson's work appears in the November 2011 issue of *The Atlantic*, in advance of the publication of *The Social Conquest of Earth*. This text, Wilson tells the interviewer, "starts with posing the questions that I call the most fundamental of philosophy and religion. Where did we come from, what are we, and where are we going?"[11] He finds answers to those questions by investigating "how roughly two dozen known examples in the history of life—humans, wasps, termites, platypodid ambrosia beetles, bathyergid mole rats, gall-making aphids, one type of snapping shrimp, and others—made the breakthrough to life in highly social, complex societies."[12] Both *The Social Conquest of Earth* and its sequel, *The Meaning of Human Existence*, are intended to combine Wilson's

10. McFarland, *From Nothing*.
11. French, "E. O. Wilson's Theory of Everything," para. 36.
12. French, "E. O. Wilson's Theory of Everything," para. 39.

research in sociobiology with the epistemological framework of universal Darwinism first developed in *Consilience*.

In *Consilience*, Wilson presents an argument for a universal account of human knowledge grounded in evolutionary theory—an account that is applicable to all aspects of human activity, from art to psychology to politics. At the heart of *Consilience* is the idea that "all tangible phenomena, from the birth of stars to the workings of social institutions, are based on material processes that are ultimately reducible, however long and torturous the sequences, to the laws of physics" and that "the unique qualities of the human species will make sense only when linked in causal explanation to the natural sciences."[13] Wilson's position is that the order of the world should be read solely through the lens of biological materialism. This natural order should then be applied to all explorations and descriptions of human nature, regardless of the usual methodologies associated with a particular discipline.[14] The goal of the consilience project extends beyond mere description into the realm of explanation, but intentionally or not, it slides frequently into moral and political prescription as well.

In Wilson's universal Darwinian schema, time exists primarily as a multiscale variable that he explains with a circuitous appeal to chaos theory. A more compact explanation of time's function in *Consilience* might look at the difference between a human being and a fruit fly. A fruit fly has a much shorter life span (or characteristic time) than a person. Thus, it is possible for a person to watch many generations of fruit flies being born, mating, and dying. At the same time, one human being cannot observe other humans in the same manner, since all humans have similar characteristic times. Wilson asks the reader to imagine herself transported to a vantage point from which the most hyper-expanded time scale ("evolutionary time") is observable. Here, one would see many generations of other human beings being born, bearing children, and dying:

> A century of their time collapses into a minute of ours. Some of their genes are changing, in both kind and relative frequency. Detached from other human beings and shorn of their emotions, godlike at last, we witness the world in evolutionary time and space.[15]

13. Wilson, *Consilience*, 292.

14. Wilson, *Consilience*, 292–93.

15. Wilson, *Consilience*, 90.

This all-encompassing viewpoint strives to keep the evolutionary time-scale perspective close at hand, so that "explanations can be joined in space from molecule to ecosystem, and in time from microsecond to millennium."[16] For Wilson, the more sweeping the perspective, in space and in time, the more helpful it is to human beings in their quest to understand the world, and to add to the ever-progressing state of human knowledge. Here, "the archaic world of myth and passion is perceived as it truly is," while "every contour of the terrain, every plant and animal living in it, and the human intellect that masters them all, can be understood more completely as a physical entity."[17] Attention to particulars is, for Wilson, antithetical to the project of knowledge—and, not uncoincidentally, of human mastery.

Wilson takes pains to emphasize that he is *not quite* on the same page as Hegel. Admitting it is "unfashionable in academic circles nowadays to speak of evolutionary progress," he writes that evolutionary progress might be rehabilitated through the use of a "simple semantic distinction"[18]:

> If we mean by progress the advance toward a preset goal, such as that composed by intention in the human mind, then evolution by natural selection, which has no preset goals, is not progress. But if we mean the production through time of increasingly complex and controlling organisms and societies, in at least some lines of descent, with regression always a possibility, then evolutionary progress is an obvious reality. In this second sense, the human attainment of high intelligence and culture ranks as the last of the four great steps in the overall history of life.[19]

For Wilson, then, progress has a *telos*, albeit one that is not "preset." At the same time, however, like the proponents of Big History, he posits some features of culture—including the culture that has produced the scientific inquiry that in turn generates universal Darwinian consilience—as the mark of the latest stage in evolution's progress.

In this story of human progress governed by evolution, not everyone can win, and not everyone should win. There is an inevitable and desirable amount of collateral damage inflicted in the "passage through evolutionary time"—damage he invites the reader to view from a godlike perspective. "Detached from other human beings" and "shorn of their emotions,"

16. Wilson, *Consilience*, 258.
17. Wilson, *Consilience*, 258.
18. Wilson, *Consilience*, 107.
19. Wilson, *Consilience*, 107.

it is far easier to ignore the individual tragedies of natural selection, as it ensures that "gene mutants that caused disease or infertility [are] weeded out in each generation."[20] But while natural selection has done the historical work of weeding out the evolutionary losers, the winners in the story of progress reading *Consilience* may rejoice in their ever-increasing self-confidence and self-sufficiency:

> The legacy of the Enlightenment is the belief that entirely on our own we can know, and in knowing, understand, and in understanding, choose wisely. That self-confidence has risen with the exponential growth of scientific knowledge, which is being woven into an increasingly full explanatory web of cause and effect. In the course of the enterprise, we have learned a great deal about ourselves as a species. We now better understand where humanity came from, and what it is. *Homo sapiens*, like the rest of life, was self-assembled.[21]

For Wilson, human progress has been the means by which humanity has gained a true knowledge of itself as self-made, self-procreated beings. This comprehension has come about thanks to the winnowing process of natural selection.[22]

Staying on the topic of biological as well as intellectual procreation, *Consilience* also addresses the relationships between human beings, both in families and in larger groups. Families, in Wilson's narration, are most likely to succeed (in the evolutionary sense) in situations of material abundance. Cooperation among members of the same family tends to reinforce the family's position of wealth, once established, and that familial solidarity is rewarded by natural selection.[23] While family relationships are described in terms of cooperation, in the case of larger social groups this cooperation between individuals is replaced by collective action, where individual bodies may be sacrificed for the good of the group:

> There is a hereditary selective advantage to membership in a powerful group united by devout belief and purpose. Even when individuals subordinate themselves and risk death in common cause, their genes are more likely to be transmitted to the next generation

20. Wilson, *Consilience*, 300.
21. Wilson, *Consilience*, 325.
22. See chapter 1.
23. Wilson, *Consilience*, 212.

than are those of competing groups who lack equivalent resolve. The individual pays, his genes and tribe gain, altruism spreads.[24]

In Wilson's account of the evolutionary role of groups viewed from the evolutionary time-scale, particular, currently existing human beings become the fertilizer of a well-organized group's future.[25]

In the final chapter, Wilson moves from philosophy to ethics, and from history to prognostication of the human future. Here, the politics that already existed within his project emerge into full view. In the future, he predicts, several trends will emerge. The first of these is increasing scarcity, as the ecosystem runs out of potentialities to be exploited: "the natural environment steadily shrinks, offering correspondingly less and less per capita return in energy and resources."[26] The second is that "within a few decades," humans will be able to "alter the biological nature of the human species in any direction . . . or leave it alone. [G]enetic evolution is about to become conscious and volitional, and usher in a new epoch in the history of life."[27]

The third trend presents, by far, the gravest danger to the human future in Wilson's worldview: overpopulation. The fear of too many people poses a mythical threat in his story, turning human beings into a looming, destructive beast, where "population growth can justly be called the monster on the land."[28] His proposed course of action to combat this beast is all too familiar: the surveillance and control of procreation. The self-procreated human becomes the human who controls the procreation of others, especially those who can be portrayed as a bestial human flood. The chapter—and the book—reach a dramatic climax in the contention that the only way to prevent an apocalyptic ecological crisis and the extinction of human life is to enforce an almost unprecedented project of state-mandated population reduction:

> Let us suppose that the last of the old reproductive taboos fade, and family planning becomes universal. Suppose further that governments create population policies with the same earnestness they devote to economic and military policies. And that as a result the global population peaks below ten billion and starts to decline. With NPG (negative population growth) attained, there

24. Wilson, *Consilience*, 282.
25. See chapter 2.
26. Wilson, *Consilience*, 296.
27. Wilson, *Consilience*, 296.
28. Wilson, *Consilience*, 315.

are grounds for hope. If not attained, humanity's best efforts will fail, and the bottleneck will close to form a solid wall.[29]

Another consequence of Wilson's "godlike" view from above is that it becomes easy to portray human beings as monolithic natural phenomena, populations stretching across time and space who in turn must be controlled en masse.

By Eternal Laws of Iron Ruled: Ernst Haeckel

Wilson is far from unique as a scientific figure whose political and philosophical writings were treated as equally authoritative as their professional contributions. The same transfer of scientific authority to the authority to explain the "meaning of human existence" and prescribe a vision for human life together can be seen in the writings of Darwin's German counterpart, Ernst Haeckel. As Daston and Galison argue, Haeckel functioned as something of a transitional or liminal figure in the development of nineteenth-century norms of scientific authority. As a scientist and a public figure, Haeckel existed within them and was formed by them, but at the same time his affinity for romanticism also placed him in relation to a previous era. Haeckel's philosophical and aesthetic sympathies added to his appeal as well as his aura of authority, "framed by the opposition between objective science and subjective art" as "an artist in scientist's clothing.[30]

Daston and Gallison draw a connection between Haeckel and Goethe that is more than just a theoretical vehicle. Haeckel explicitly situated himself, and his work, in the lineage of Goethe. His philosophical treatise, *The Riddle of the Universe at the Close of the Nineteenth Century*, which shares many features with *Consilience*, ends with an evocation of the poet. Haeckel writes,

> Germany's greatest thinker and poet . . . Wolfgang Goethe . . . gave this "philosophy of unity" a perfect poetic expression, at the very beginning of this century, in his immortal poems, *Faust, Prometheus*, and *God and the World*:
> "By eternal laws
> Of iron ruled,
> Must all fulfill

---

29. Wilson, *Consilience*, 315–16.
30. Daston and Galison, *Objectivity*, 247.

The cycle of
Their destiny."[31]

Just as in Wilson's later project of universal Darwinism, the destiny that
Haeckel has in mind throughout the text proves to be far from universal.
Instead, it is based on a very particular, and particularly German, vision of
the *telos* of the unfolding process of the history of the world.

The Riddle of the Universe begins as a work of descriptive evolutionary biology, tracing a trajectory of biological development for the human
species. But the text quickly reveals the much more ambitious extent of
Haeckel's project, describing the development of consciousness under the
same evolutionary schema before moving to its explicitly normative content. Like Wilson, Haeckel is hostile to Christianity, and proposes to replace
Christian faith, ethical norms, and ecclesial structures with a properly progressive alternative: the "religion" of monism and an anthropology that fits
within its worldview.[32]

This development quickly travels into the realm of the political. As
Haeckel explains, one of the principal benefits of monistic anthropology is
that it will free "the cultured State" from the "absolute submission" required
of it by Christianity—or at least by a Catholicism that claimed authority
over the rulers of nations. Haeckel's words may call to mind contemporary
American rhetoric around the teaching of evolution and creationism, but
the conflict between science and Christianity he describes has as much to
do with the context of Bismarck's political battles with the claims of papal
authority as it does with epistemology or education:

> Either the Church wins, and then farewell to all "free science and
> free teaching"—then our universities no better than jails, and our
> colleges become cloistral schools; or else the modern rational State
> proves victorious—then, in the twentieth century, human culture,
> freedom, and prosperity will continue their progressive devel-
> opment until they far surpass even the height of the nineteenth
> century.[33]

In terms that echo the most unfortunate aspects of contemporary American
rhetoric, Haeckel contrasts Christian faith (or, more accurately, a caricature
of it) with an alternative governed by scientific reason. Yet the "modern

31. Haeckel, *Riddle of the Universe*, 383.
32. Haeckel, *Riddle of the Universe*, 331.
33. Haeckel, *Riddle of the Universe*, 335–36.

BEYOND

rational State" he hopes to see triumph in this clash of cultures is a far-from-innocuous concept.

Haeckel's alternative is a biological form of natural theology that places science and scientists in the position of authority—and in the position of transparency to reason. As he writes,

> The paths which lead to the noble divinity of truth and knowledge are the loving study of nature and its laws, the observation of the infinitely great star-world with the aid of the telescope, and the infinitely tiny cell-world with the aid of the microscope—not senseless ceremonies and unthinking prayers, not alms and Peter's Pence.[34]

In Haeckel's estimation, Christianity was a necessary stage in human development, but it is one that humanity is now poised—and, indeed, required—to progress beyond.

At the same time, it becomes clear his objection to Christianity is not based on its beliefs as such, but on the content of its political and moral claims:

> In the great *cultur-kampf*, which must go on as long as these sad conditions exist, the first aim must be absolute separation of Church and State. There shall be "a free Church in a free State"—that is, every Church shall be free in the practice of its special worship and ceremonies, and in the construction of its fantastic poetry and superstitious dogmas—with the sole condition that they contain no danger to social order or morality.[35]

Nowhere is this more evident than in his critique of the Sermon on the Mount (Matt 5):

> One of the Christian precepts that were impressed upon us in our early youth as of great importance, and that are glorified in millions of sermons, is: "Love your enemies, bless them that curse you, do good to them that hate you, and pray for them which despitefully use you and persecute you." It is a very ideal precept, but as useless in practice as it is unnatural. So it is with the counsel, "If any man take away thy coat, let him have thy cloak also." Translated into the terms of modern life, that means: "When some unscrupulous scoundrel has defrauded thee of half thy goods, let him have the other half also." Or, again, in the language of modern

34. Haeckel, *Riddle of the Universe*, 337.
35. Haeckel, *Riddle of the Universe*, 360–61.

politics: "When the pious English take from you simple Germans one after another of your valuable colonies in Africa, let them have all the rest of your colonies also—or, best of all, give them Germany itself."[36]

Haeckel is inadvertently correct in that love of enemies is precisely neither natural nor useful, and that it is a mark of Christian discipleship rather than a universal moral edict. However, his deployment of German colonialism as the obviously "natural" counterexample reveals the depth to which nationalist ideology pervades his thought.

At the height of the First World War, Haeckel would again return to the question of Germany's colonial aspirations in Africa. As a prominent public supporter of Kaiser Wilhelm's war aims from the start of the conflict, he signed the 1914 statement of German intellectuals "To the Civilized World," defending the invasion of Belgium.[37] Two years later, an excerpt from his book, *Eternity: World-War Thoughts on Life and Death, Religion, and the Theory of Evolution,* appeared in the *New York Times* for the benefit of American readers. Under the headline "Ernst Haeckel Gives Germany's Peace Terms," it was published with this introductory editorial note:

> Professor Ernst Haeckel, the German exponent of evolutionary principles and the contemporary of Darwin, Wallace, and Spencer, has for a long time espoused the cause of international solidarity and peace. At the beginning of the war his voice, like that of many other German intellectuals, was raised bitterly against England. Professor Haeckel has just written a book called "Eternity: World-War Thoughts on Life and Death, Religion, and the Theory of Evolution," in which he discusses terms of peace that he believes would be acceptable to Germany. The book shows in some degree the sobering effect of time. It will soon be published in English by The Truth Seeker Company in a translation by Thomas Seltzer, translator of Oswald's "Natural Philosophy"; who prepared the following excerpts for *The New York Times*.[38]

This presentation of Haeckel as an authoritative voice of German reason was intensified by the inclusion of a large engraved portrait with the article. The image shows Haeckel as a rugged elder statesman, with an evocative facial expression that conveys wisdom and equanimity. The cumulative effect

36. Haeckel, *Riddle of the Universe,* 353–54.
37. "To the Civilized World, by Professors of Germany."
38. Haeckel, "Ernst Haeckel Gives Germany's Peace Terms," para. 1.

of image and text is consonant with the *Times'* 1916 editorial position of Wilsonian neutrality. If the German cause could be presented as eminently reasonable, then America would have no need to enter the war on the side of Britain and France.

Haeckel's text, as translated and reprinted in the American press, bears quoting at length. The heart of his message was that "we [Germany] must demand a considerable extension of the German Empire," and his rhetoric in delivering that ultimatum is noteworthy. He opens with an appeal to the "higher civilized nations" for cooperation and comity:

> Our aim is to prevent the inevitable but bloodless 'competitive struggle' from degenerating into a bloody and murderous 'struggle for existence.' The higher civilized nations should exercise mutual tolerance toward each other and combine for higher common cultural work in the service of true humanity.[39]

The devil, as always, emerges in the details of the proposed arrangement between the European powers:

> [T]he German Empire, being overpopulated, has urgent need to extend and strengthen its frontiers . . . It needs this, first, in order to secure itself against future attacks of our stronger neighbors; and, second, in order not to lose the large numbers of German citizens who emigrate yearly from the narrow confines of the Fatherland to serve as "cultural manure" for other countries. The new provinces which we are going to annex are energetic and reckless, but with cautious and intelligent treatment they can be Germanized, or at least made accessible to German culture, education, and civilization.[40]

Haeckel continues by calling not only for an expansion of the borders of the *metropole*, of Germany proper, but also of German colonies in Africa:

> This all-embracing world war has taught us many important lessons. One of them, which is of special importance, is the growing conviction that the German Empire as a world power needs extensive colonies . . . Of the various proposals recently made for the extension of the colonies which we have already acquired, the one that holds out the best promise is the foundation of a great German colonial empire in middle Africa . . . In adding the Congo to our colonies in the eastern and western part of middle Africa,

39. Haeckel, "Ernst Haeckel Gives Germany's Peace Terms," para. 6.
40. Haeckel, "Ernst Haeckel Gives Germany's Peace Terms," para. 9.

which as a result of tremendous efforts on our part have already reached a high degree of prosperity, we shall have a vast region, the exploitation of which by the energy, industry, knowledge and intelligence of German colonists promises a most profitable field for us for centuries to come.[41]

Here, Haeckel echoes the prevalent German conventional wisdom of the day, which tied anxiety over its existence as a relatively new nation to the desire for colonial possessions to match those of other European powers. Peaceable coexistence between the European powers, then, would be predicated on Germany's ability to rival Britain and France as colonial states.

The *Times* excerpt closes with a rhetorically stirring—and philosophically astonishing—paean to human progress:

> Considering the magnificent strides that the idea of evolution has made in the course of the last half-century in all branches of human knowledge, we feel reasonably confident that it will also succeed in leading suffering mankind out of the chaos of the present insane world war up to a higher stage of civilization and happiness. ... Standing on the high watch tower of pure reason and surveying the world in general, I am moved to express the desire that the recognized principles of pure morality which civilized men have for a long time striven to follow in their narrow personal relations to each other should also become the norm within the State, guiding the conduct of the different social classes toward each other, and also the international relations between the different States. . . . Proceeding from the realistic point of view of our monistic natural philosophy, we recognize in the present world catastrophe rather one of those turning points in the history of mankind at which, under the combined weight of prodigious progress and incisive chance, there will arise out of the "good old times" new forms of national life.[42]

There is much to explore in this remarkable passage that lies outside the scope of this book. For now, two points are especially worth noting. The first is Haeckel's belief that "the idea of evolution" is the ground of humanity's hope for an end to the current war, as well as for progress to a "higher stage of civilization." The second, which proceeds from the first, is that Haeckel positions himself as a (if not the) clear-sighted authority, who from "the high watch tower of pure reason" is uniquely qualified to make

41. Haeckel, "Ernst Haeckel Gives Germany's Peace Terms," paras. 15 and 18.
42. Haeckel, "Ernst Haeckel Gives Germany's Peace Terms," para. 20.

normative moral and political prescriptions for "the world in general." Not only does Haeckel stand in the position of transparency to reason to evaluate the time, he also positions himself as the authority who can guide the present into the future.

Becoming an I-I

The Earth Is Round

In Wilson's theory of consilience, as in Haeckel's all-encompassing theory of monism, science functions as the authoritative source of a system that explains and governs all of existence, with scientific man as the progenitor and proclaimer of that system. And yet, as Julia Watkin points out in her commentary on Kierkegaard's *Concluding Unscientific Postscript*, this logic makes the mistake of confusing objective description with the subjective human predicament. Popularizers of science, she writes, tend to go "beyond using a system constructed logically on the basis of principles derived from induction and mathematics" and to "the creation of an existential system."[43] Wilson and Haeckel may begin from the standpoint of their biological expertise, but the migration of their thought to questions of meaning and political projects is a common and perhaps even inevitable category error.

Writing under the pseudonym of Johannes Climacus, Kierkegaard illustrates this category error with the whimsical tale of an escapee from the madhouse who tries (and fails) to prove his sanity by an inappropriately deployed appeal to objective truth:

> What [he needs] to do, then, is to convince everyone completely, by the objective truth of what [he says], that all is well as far as [his] sanity is concerned. As he is walking along and pondering this, he sees a skittle ball lying on the ground. He picks it up and puts it in the tail of his coat. At every step he takes, this ball bumps him, if you please, on his r——, and every time it bumps him he says, "Boom! The earth is round." He arrives in the capital city and immediately visits one of his friends. He wants to convince him that he is not lunatic and therefore paces up and down the floor and continually says, "Boom! The earth is round!" But is the earth not round? Does the madhouse demand yet another sacrifice on account of this assumption, as in those days when everyone assumed it to be as flat as a pancake? Or is he lunatic, the man who hopes to

43. Watkin, "Boom! The Earth Is Round!," 108.

prove that he is not lunatic by stating a truth universally accepted and universally regarded as objective? And yet, precisely by this it became clear to the physician that the patient was not yet cured, although the cure certainly could not revolve around getting him to assume that the earth is flat.[44]

Climacus's example here is comedic, but it illustrates succinctly the error that scientists, and particularly evolutionary scientists, stumble into as their thought drifts into matters of human meaning and human life together. The operative problem with Haeckel and Wilson's thought is not the truth or falsehood of evolutionary biology in itself. Rather, it is their assertion of scientific objectivity in an attempt to explain truths that biology cannot, in fact, explain. As Kierkegaard might suggest, the cure for this problem has nothing to do with reasserting the reading of the creation narratives that is often dubbed "creationism" in contemporary American debates. The earth is not flat. But shouting its roundness in the street makes the shouter a comic figure, and not an authoritative explainer of the meaning of human existence.

In teaching seminary students how to think about evolutionary theory, I often use the example of Ohm's Law from introductory physics. It is uncontroversially true that voltage in an electric circuit is proportional to current and resistance: $V=IR$. Likewise, it is uncontroversially true that evolutionary theory has something to say about how species develop and differentiate themselves from each other, even if the exact mechanism of that differentiation is still contested. But that biological truth—the earth's roundness, as it were—should have as little hold on the moral imagination as Ohm's Law does. Electricity is everywhere, but no one believes that Ohm's law explains the poverty of Haiti or the pitfalls of marriage. Popular accounts of evolutionary biology, however, have been far less circumspect in the limits of its explanatory power.

Elevated Calm and Comical Thoughtlessness

I do not mean to suggest that scientific inquiry and the scientific method cannot be a vital part of the intellectual life. For Johannes Climacus, such thought may be "wholly legitimate" in its proper place.[45] The problem, he argues, arises when the "inquiring, speculating, knowing subject" is one

---

44. Kierkegaard, *Concluding Unscientific Postscript*, 1:195.

45. Kierkegaard, *Concluding Unscientific Postscript*, 1:25.

who "asks about the truth but not about the subjective truth, the truth of appropriation."[46] This "inquiring subject" is "indeed interested but is not infinitely, passionately, impassionedly interested in his relation to truth concerning his own eternal happiness"[47] He continues,

> Let the scientific researcher labor with restless zeal, let him even shorten his life in the enthusiastic service of science and scholarship; let the speculative thinker spare neither time nor effort— they are nevertheless not infinitely, personally, impassionedly interested. On the contrary, they do not want to be. Their observations will be objective, disinterested. With regard to the subject's relation to known truth, it is assumed that if only the objective truth has been obtained, appropriation is an easy matter; it is automatically included as part of the bargain, and *am Ende* [in the end] the individual is a matter of indifference. Precisely this is the basis of the scholar's elevated calm and the parroter's comical thoughtlessness.[48]

This "elevated" position of speculation leaves no room for involvement with the thinker's own situation. Here, there is no room for what Kierkegaard customarily refers to as the "subjective" stance—which in his writing has to do with the individual's engagement with, and appropriation of, thought from within daily life.

The ramifications of this position become clear as Climacus engages directly with G. W. F. Hegel and his attempts to generate an encyclopedic and all-encompassing system of being and knowledge. "Existence," he writes, "is the spacing that holds apart," but "the systematic is the conclusiveness that combines."[49] Who, Climacus asks, is the one who thinks systematically in this way? It is none other than God. Those who would place themselves in the position of system-building catapult themselves into the place of God, where they can observe and evaluate the world from God's perspective. Climacus explains that "he who himself is outside existence and yet in existence, who in his eternity is forever concluded and yet includes existence within himself—it is God."[50]

46. Kierkegaard, *Concluding Unscientific Postscript*, 1:21.
47. Kierkegaard, *Concluding Unscientific Postscript*, 1:21.
48. Kierkegaard, *Concluding Unscientific Postscript*, 1:21.
49. Kierkegaard, *Concluding Unscientific Postscript*, 1:118.
50. Kierkegaard, *Concluding Unscientific Postscript*, 1:119.

Just as in the fragmentary biography *Johannes Climacus*, systematic thought is described in comedic terms. One of Kierkegaard's characteristic moves is to make the system-builder a comic figure worthy of gentle ridicule. Climacus, in turn, does much the same in *Concluding Unscientific Postscript*:

> It follows that such a thinker must be either the good Lord or a fantastical *quodlibet* [anything]. Certainly everyone will perceive the immorality in this, and certainly everyone will also perceive that what another author has observed regarding the Hegelian system is entirely in order: that through Hegel a system, the absolute system, was brought to completion—without having an ethics. By all means, let us smile at the ethical-religious fantasies of the Middle Ages in asceticism and the like, but above all let us not forget that the speculative, farcical exaggeration of becoming an I-I—and then *qua* human being often such a philistine that no enthusiast would have cared to lead such a life—is equally ludicrous.[51]

As Julia Watkin has noted, and as Amy Laura Hall and I have described in another essay, the self-positing I-I who places herself outside existence loses herself, and the possibility of ethics, in the process. She writes,

> Loss of contact with ethics occurs firstly through the thinker's make-believe standpoint in which he or she takes some fantastical God's-eye position outside the universe, that is, outside existence. Since objective thinking, in that it concerns description of the world, has no relation to the individual thinker's personal life, daily life becomes an inconvenient appendage to the great work of System-building (*CUP*, 1:119, 122–23). Secondly, there is a loss of ethics in the Hegelian-style System because it contains ethics and morality as a necessary process. Yet in a necessary process there can be no freedom and hence no ethics.[52]

The detachment Watkin names here is also related to another feature of Hegelianism that Climacus describes in *Concluding Unscientific Postscript*: looking at time in terms of the sweep of world history.

As Climacus writes in the chapter on "Becoming Subjective," the danger in looking at time from a perspective that encompasses all of world history lies precisely in its allure to the thinker:

---

51. Kierkegaard, *Concluding Unscientific Postscript*, 1:119–20.
52. Watkin, "Boom! The Earth Is Round!," 101.

Therefore ethics looks with a suspicious eye at all world-historical knowledge, because this easily becomes a trap, a demoralizing esthetic diversion for the knowing subject, because the distinction between what does and does not become world-historical is quantitative-dialectical. That is also why the absolute ethical distinction between good and evil is world-historically-esthetically neutralized in the esthetic-metaphysical category of "the great," "the momentous," to which the bad and the good have equal access. In the world-historical, an essential role is played by factors of another kind, different from the ethical-dialectical: namely, the accidental, circumstances, that play of forces in which the reshaping totality of historical life absorbs the individual's action in order to transform it into something different that does not directly belong to him. Neither by willing the good to the utmost of his ability nor by willing evil with diabolical callousness is a person assured of becoming world-historical; even in the case of misfortune, it holds true that it takes luck to become world-historical. How, then, does an individual become world-historical? Ethically viewed, he becomes world-historical by accident. But ethics also considers unethical the transition whereby a person abandons the ethical quality in order to try his hand, cravingly, wishfully, etc., at the quantifying other.[53]

Climacus does much in this passage to confuse himself, and perhaps his reader as well. But he is clear insofar as he connects world-historical thought to the tendency to evaluate the significance of events in time, and to ascribe necessity in retrospect to those things that are, in fact, a product of accident, chance, or contingency. And he is also clear that this tendency is related to the impulse to quantify one's neighbors, to view them *en masse* rather than as unique neighbors.

Alluding to Hegel's ordering of temporal geography in the *Philosophy of History*, Climacus also notes the ways that the speculative, world-historical view from above is deployed. In his discussion, "China" stands in for all of the non-German territories that are placed somehow outside of the present in the Hegelian system. As he playfully writes,

> Would that I could display scholarship at this point! Would that I could show how the authorized and yet *valore intrinseco* [according to its intrinsic worth] rather dubious Hegelian ordering of the world-historical process depends upon arbitrariness and leaps, how China ought to be assigned another place and a new

53. Kierkegaard, *Concluding Unscientific Postscript*, 1:134.

paragraph be inserted for a recently discovered tribe in Monomotapa; would that I could show how the Hegelian method looks
almost like a prank when it is used on a minor detail—then perhaps I could satisfy some reader. That is, the interest in ordering
the world-historical would remain essential, but what I said about
Monomotapa would be impressive, just as Jeronimus is impressed
by what the schoolmaster in Julestuen says about the phoenix bird
native to Arabia.[54]

He elaborates on this point in a footnote that is telling in its connection of
academic ambition to the political particularity of European scholarship,
where "the method admits only one Chinese, but not a single German assistant professor is excluded, especially no Prussian, because whoever has
the cross blesses himself first."[55] The system may acknowledge China and its
people only as tokens of futurity, but all Germans are included as a matter
of right.

In addition, the act of viewing time from above to evaluate its significance can tempt the viewer towards trying to become significant in herself
and through her own actions:

> An age and a person can be immoral in various ways, but it is also
> immoral or at least a temptation to consort too much with world
> history, a temptation that can easily lead a person to want also to be
> world-historical when the time comes that he himself is going to
> act. By continually being occupied as an observer of the acciden-
> tal, that *accessorium* [addition] by which world-historical figures
> become world-historical, a person is easily misled into confusing
> this *accessorium* with the ethical and easily misled, unhealthily,
> flirtingly, and cowardly, to being concerned about the accidental,
> instead, himself existing, of being infinitely concerned about the
> ethical. Perhaps the reason our age is dissatisfied when it is going
> to act is that it has been coddled by observing. That is perhaps why
> there are so many fruitless attempts to become something more
> than one is by lumping together socially in the hope of impressing
> the spirit of history numerically. Spoiled by constant association
> with world history, people want the momentous and only that, are
> concerned only with the accidental, the world-historical outcome,
> instead of being concerned with the essential, the innermost, free-
> dom, the ethical.[56]

54. Kierkegaard, *Concluding Unscientific Postscript*, 1:150.
55. Kierkegaard, *Concluding Unscientific Postscript*, 1:188.
56. Kierkegaard, *Concluding Unscientific Postscript*, 1:135.

The drive to make a mark on the trajectory of world history, and indeed to direct its course, may look like ethics but is antithetical to it. The alternative is to hold one's own importance lightly while treating God with the utmost seriousness, "willing to the utmost of one's capability, but also, uplifted in divine jest, in never thinking whether or not one thereby achieves something."[57] If one were to look for ethics, one would find it not in a stance of moral and historical heroism but in awareness of both the absurdity and the seriousness of the human condition.

A Rash Anticipation

The reality of human sin, and the depth to which Kierkegaard treats its acknowledgment as intrinsic to the Christian life, appears obliquely and tellingly in Climacus's repeated allusions to Johannes de Silentio and the text of *Fear and Trembling*. In a significant aside, Climacus writes:

> But is humor the incognito of the religious person? Is not his incognito this, that there is nothing whatever to be noticed, nothing at all that could arouse suspicion of the hidden inwardness, not even so much as the humoristic? At its very maximum, if this could be reached in existence, this would no doubt be so;* yet as long as the struggle and the suffering in inwardness continue he will not succeed in hiding his inwardness completely, but he will not express it directly, and he will hinder it negatively with the aid of the humorous.[58]

Is the Christian alternative to claims of world-historical significance approached through a form of humor that is itself a form of giving birth to the self—a philosophical performance of the sort seen in the comic nihilism of *South Park*? The asterisk in Climacus' passage above leads to yet another parenthetical remark. He writes,

> In *Fear and Trembling*, a "knight of faith" such as this was portrayed. But this portrayal was only a rash anticipation, and the illusion was gained by depicting him in a state of completeness, and hence in a false medium, instead of in the existence-medium, and the beginning was made by ignoring the contradiction—how an observer could become at all aware of him in such a way that he could place himself, admiring, outside and admire that there is

---

57. Kierkegaard, *Concluding Unscientific Postscript*, 1:135.
58. Kierkegaard, *Concluding Unscientific Postscript*, 1:500–1.

nothing, nothing whatever, to notice, unless Johannes de Silentio would say that the knight of faith is his own poetic production.[59]

Sin is the missing ingredient in De Silentio's construction of the knight of faith, and sin is what prevents any would-be knight from propelling themselves into a poetic leap of faith. The question of sin and the human condition is also one of the subjects of *Philosophical Fragments*, which also appears under the pseudonym of Johannes Climacus. In *Concluding Unscientific Postscript*, Climacus alludes to the existing thinker as one who is "never a teacher, but a learner, and if he is continually just as negative as positive, he is continually striving."[60] Climacus continues, "Greek philosophy had a continual relation to ethics. That was why continually wanting to be a learner was not regarded as a great discovery or the inspired undertaking of an exceptional individual, since it was neither more nor less than the understanding that one is existing and that to be conscious of this is no merit but to forget it is thoughtlessness."[61]

How this learning comes about is not a matter of self-generation, but of the gift that we receive by means of the descent that is the incarnation. As Climacus writes in *Philosophical Fragments*,

> The teacher, then, is the god himself, who, acting as the occasion, prompts the learner to be reminded that he is untruth and is that through his own fault. But this state—to be untruth and to be that through one's own fault—what can we call it? Let us call it *sin* . . . What, then, should we call such a teacher who gives him the condition again and along with it the truth? Let us call him a savior, for he does indeed save the learner from unfreedom, saves him from himself. Let us call him a deliverer, for he does indeed deliver the person who had imprisoned himself, and no one is so dreadfully imprisoned, and no captivity is so impossible to break out of as that in which the individual holds himself captive! And yet, even this does not say enough, for by his unfreedom he had indeed become guilty of something, and if that teacher gives him the condition and the truth, then he is, of course, a reconciler who takes away the wrath that lay over the incurred guilt.[62]

59. Kierkegaard, *Concluding Unscientific Postscript*, 1:586.
60. Kierkegaard, *Concluding Unscientific Postscript*, 1:85.
61. Kierkegaard, *Concluding Unscientific Postscript*, 1:122.
62. Kierkegaard, *Philosophical Fragments*, 15, 17.

This is the occasion for what Climacus describes as the "moment" by which one learns the truth about themselves—the meaning of human existence:

> A moment such as this is unique. To be sure, it is short and temporal, as the moment is; it is passing, as the moment is, past, as the moment is in the next moment, and yet it is decisive, and yet it is filled with the eternal. A moment such as this must have a special name. Let us call it: the fullness of time.[63]

The fullness of time is not to be seized, instrumentalized, or evaluated from a distance. The fullness of time comes in the person of the Savior, the Word made flesh. The fullness of time reveals human sin, even as it overwhelms that sin in freedom and grace.

The Body of Weakness

Let us return briefly to the world of consilience, where "explanations can be joined in space from molecule to ecosystem, and in time from microsecond to millennium."[64] In his celebration of human progress and human potential, Wilson closely resembles another paradigmatic man, one who was described by Karl Barth as "free from all ties of tradition and all conflict with tradition, who rejoices equally in reason and in history . . . the man [who] for the first time achieved complete, clear, and certain self-awareness"[65] He is the man who "cannot understand himself more deeply, more exactly, more definitely, than simply as thinking man. It is in thinking and in thinking alone that he is different from the animals, that he is, as man, himself."[66] This is Barth's portrait of the human subject in the work of G. W. F. Hegel.

Writing in *Protestant Theology of the Nineteenth Century*, Barth explains it was the most "characteristically modern" aspect of Hegel that he "dared to want to invent such a method, a key to open every lock, a lever to set every wheel working at once, an observation tower from which not only all the lands of the earth, but the third and seventh heavens, too, can be surveyed at a glance."[67] The logic here at work in Hegel is not only a logic of seeing, or even of evaluating the significance of history. As Kierkegaard

---

63. Kierkegaard, *Philosophical Fragments*, 18.
64. Wilson, *Consilience*, 258.
65. Barth, *Protestant Theology of the Nineteenth Century*, 371.
66. Barth, *Protestant Theology of the Nineteenth Century*, 384.
67. Barth, *Protestant Theology of the Nineteenth Century*, 392.

would suggest repeatedly, it is also a logic of aspiring to significance for oneself. If I can see the sweep of all that is and all that has been, the logical next step is to try to control what will be. And here, too, Barth can provide a helpful contrary word.

In *Church Dogmatics* I/2, Barth repeatedly draws a distinction between man and flesh, between a heroic ideal of Christ and the reality of revelation. In the incarnation, he writes, Jesus "not merely bore the body, but the body of weakness," and "not merely the being of man but the actual being of the entire solid poverty of cosmic impotence, the entire limitations of fleshly being."[68] It is precisely in this way, in the "divine realism" of becoming flesh, that as the second Adam, Christ "made good what Adam perverted."[69] His sinlessness, then, cannot and does not "consist in an ethical heroism, but precisely in a renunciation of any heroism, including the ethical. He is sinless not in spite of, but just because of his being the friend of publicans and sinners and His dying between the malefactors."[70] Contrary to what many texts on Christian leadership may argue, the *imitatio Christi* looks like the opposite of strength. The extent to which Christians rely on their strength to achieve a heroic ideal reveals their sinfulness, rather than their success in discipleship. The incarnation, as the event that truly did turn the world upside-down, is the one event that rejects any human attempt to seize the wheel of history and turn it. What God does, human beings cannot.

Eternal Laws of Iron

We have already seen how Ernst Haeckel cited Goethe's "eternal laws of iron" to argue for a particular form of scientific determinism and a particular teleological vision of human progress. Writing in *Church Dogmatics* III/3, Barth cites the same lines as he engages with the role of scientific laws within his doctrine of creation. For Barth, scientific laws are valid and have their place, but they cannot be invoked in order to say something about God or about divine providence. Rather, the two must be kept clearly separated:

> Hypothetically—and even Christians will not cease to do it—we can reckon with the fact that there are such things as the so-called unbreakable and unbroken external physical laws, i.e., laws which in human experience are so regular as not to admit of any

68. Barth, *Church Dogmatics* I/2, 155.
69. Barth, *Church Dogmatics* I/2, 157.
70. Barth, *Church Dogmatics* I/2, 157.

exception, and also the intellectual laws which conform to them, mathematically comprehended perhaps in a higher logicality to form a system of objective laws of being and motion in which room may well be found for a kind of moral law of nature as the norm of historical occurrence. In biblical thinking this idea plays absolutely no part at all, and in this it may be compared with the conception of a total force. But does this mean that there is any reason not to reckon with it as a hypothesis? We can still accept norms of this kind, and perhaps a sum and substance of all these norms. We can still presuppose and expect that every individual occurrence will take place within the framework of these norms and therefore as a process predetermined by law. It may still be the case that

> "According to great, eternal,
> Brazen laws,
> We must all
> Fulfil the circle
> Of our destiny." (Goethe 1783)

But even conceding that that is the case, we still cannot equate the practical validity and actuality of those laws with the divine activity which foreordains creaturely occurrence.[71]

Even in the "maximal case," physical laws do not have the "power" to "cause even the most trivial of creaturely events actually to take place."[72] Even this case is chastened by the fact that there does not exist a theory of every-thing, that "we have a knowledge not of the law of all creaturely occurrence, but of certain laws which are normative for particular fields of creaturely occurrence."[73]

For Barth, the role of science is not eliminated but circumscribed in its theological aspirations. They are "practically valid and therefore effective in all occurrence." At the same time, however, "there is also no reason to pass them off as 'eternal' or to compare or equate them with the law or laws of God." No physical law "is known to us with the certainty with which God is known to us by His Word" as the "real foreordination of creaturely occurrence."[74] In his writing on divine providence that occupies much of the third volume of his doctrine of creation, Barth is not only concerned

---

71. Barth, *Church Dogmatics* III/3, 124–25.

72. Barth, *Church Dogmatics* III/3, 125.

73. Barth, *Church Dogmatics* III/3, 126.

74. Barth, *Church Dogmatics* III/3, 127.

with the proper role of scientific principles within an apprehension of God's work in the world. In the following subparagraph, The Divine Ruling, he takes pains to emphasize that this work can never require some human beings to be sacrificed in the name of progress or of world-historical development, "rendering their service to the whole at the proper time," yet "existing only to be sacrificed at the last for the life and progress of the whole and the favoured few."[75]

Moreover, the concept of the "totality," whether creation as a whole, or humanity, or the nation, or any other group, cannot erase or elide the individual to whom God is in loving relationship as Creator to creature. God "harmonises and co-ordinates the creatures one with another," but "this does not mean that the individual creature has no meaning nor right to exist except as a non-autonomous atom, a mere cog in a machine, a functionary in a collective action, and ultimately and supremely in the one collective action of world-occurrence as a whole."[76] No individual can be "used and then dropped and trampled underfoot."[77] From eternity, God has elected not to see human beings from Wilson's godlike view. God has chosen to be for each one of us and our neighbors, in Jesus Christ.

Instead, in "the kingdom of the King," which is "a kingdom of righteousness," God "deals with each one in a direct and immediate encounter and relationship with Himself."[78] In this relationship, human beings are brought low by the reality of their condition, but they are not left in despair:

> There is not one of them which His rule does not abase, but there is also not one of them which being abased by Him is not exalted. There is not one of them which His rule does not co-ordinate and fuse with others into a single whole, but there is also not one of them which is made only to suffer by this relationship, which is not comforted and gladdened by it, seeing that God Himself created it.[79]

The creature is not God, but neither is the creature only abased in relationship with and to God. In Christ, the creature is exalted as well, but this is not a matter of self-exaltation in which the creature can place itself on high.

75. Barth, *Church Dogmatics* III/3, 173.
76. Barth, *Church Dogmatics* III/3, 169.
77. Barth, *Church Dogmatics* III/3, 173.
78. Barth, *Church Dogmatics* III/3, 173.
79. Barth, *Church Dogmatics* III/3, 173.

Rather, it is an exaltation by and through the person of Jesus Christ, who became a servant for humanity's sake and for the sake of each human being.

In the liturgical calendar, the ascension is not a self-propulsive act of humanity, but the final act of the incarnation that makes an important eschatological claim. Just as humanity does not place itself on high at the ascension, so also the return of Christ from whence he ascended cannot come from within creation as a human act. For all the difficulty that the ascension poses for modern readers, or for artists throughout the centuries who have tried to depict it, it is indispensable for precisely this eschatological reason. Without it, the kingdom of God would become a matter of human achievement, and we would thus be left at the mercy of someone else's vision of progress—or trapped within our own.

6

The Fullness of Time

So if anyone is in Christ, there is a new creation: everything old has passed
away; see, everything has become new! All this is from God, who reconciled
us to himself through Christ, and has given us the ministry of reconciliation;
that is, in Christ God was reconciling the world to himself, not counting their
trespasses against them, and entrusting the message of reconciliation to us.
So we are ambassadors for Christ, since God is making his appeal through us;
we entreat you on behalf of Christ, be reconciled to God.

—2 CORINTHIANS 5:17-20 (NRSV)

I write these words in the midst of a global pandemic that has claimed far
too many lives in my home state of New Jersey and around the world.
Those who endured the terrible spring of 2020, including myself, look to a
hopefully near time when a vaccine will be tested and manufactured. It will
be a product of scientific research, and it will be a great good. Nothing in
this book is intended to suggest otherwise. However, I have been fascinated
to see yard signs reading "I believe in science" sprouting along some local
roads. Insofar as these signs are meant to signal support of public health
measures, they are fine statements given the baffling, and potentially harmful, politicization of those measures.

However, it seems to me that for Christians to say "I believe in science" is
worth troubling in two ways. First, as I hope I have shown through historical
and contemporary examples, "science" is not a monolithic, reified, ahistorical
entity. It is a set of practices, existing within a particular context, that can

generate true descriptions of the material universe, but its practitioners are subject to the temptations to stray far beyond that remit. It is a set of practices carried out by sinful human beings, creatures trying to understand creation. Second, to say "I believe in science" can never be the same kind of statement of belief as the Nicene Creed. Scientific knowledge is real, but God is more real than that. The reality of God forms our existence in time, not through force, but as a free and gracious gift worthy of praise.

I close with a final example that I hope shows the character of Christian life in time that is shaped by the reality of God. On the feasts of Christmas and Epiphany, just twelve days apart, many Christians mark time with two acts of liturgical proclamation. The first of these is the solemn proclamation of Christmas from the Roman martyrology, which places the singular nature of the event of the incarnation within other markers of human history:

> The Twenty-fifth Day of December,
> when ages beyond number had run their course
> from the creation of the world,
> when God in the beginning created heaven and earth,
> and formed man in his own likeness;
> when century upon century had passed
> since the Almighty set his bow in the clouds after the Great Flood,
> as a sign of covenant and peace;
> in the twenty-first century since Abraham, our father in faith,
> came out of Ur of the Chaldees;
> in the thirteenth century since the People of Israel were led by Moses
> in the Exodus from Egypt;
> around the thousandth year since David was anointed King;
> in the sixty-fifth week of the prophecy of Daniel;
> in the one hundred and ninety-fourth Olympiad;
> in the year seven hundred and fifty-two
> since the foundation of the City of Rome;
> in the forty-second year of the reign of Caesar Octavian Augustus,
> the whole world being at peace,
>
> Jesus Christ, eternal God and Son of the eternal Father,
> desiring to consecrate the world by his most loving presence,
> was conceived by the Holy Spirit,
> and when nine months had passed since his conception,
> was born of the Virgin Mary in Bethlehem of Judah,
> and was made man:
>
> The Nativity of Our Lord Jesus Christ according to the flesh.[1]

---

1. United States Conference of Catholic Bishops, "Nativity of Our Lord Jesus Christ," para. 3.

Then, at Epiphany, the liturgical calendar for the following year is announced using a traditional text that calculates the liturgical year from the events of Good Friday and Easter. For example, in 2020, the Epiphany proclamation read as follows:

> Dear friends in Christ, the glory of the Lord has shone upon us, and shall ever be manifest among us, until the day of his return. Through the rhythms of times and seasons let us celebrate the mysteries of salvation. Let us recall the year's culmination, the Easter Triduum of the Lord: his last supper, his crucifixion, his burial, and his rising celebrated between the evening of the ninth day of April and the evening of the eleventh day of April.
>
> Each Easter—as on each Sunday—the Holy Church makes present the great and saving deed by which Christ has for ever conquered sin and death. From Easter are reckoned all the days we keep holy. Ash Wednesday, the beginning of Lent, will occur on the twenty-sixth day of February. The Ascension of the Lord will be commemorated on the twenty-first day of May. Pentecost, the joyful conclusion of the season of Easter, will be celebrated on the thirty-first day of May. And, this year the First Sunday of Advent will be on the twenty-ninth day of November.
>
> Likewise the pilgrim Church proclaims the passover of Christ in the feasts of the holy Mother of God, in the feasts of the Apostles and Saints, and in the commemoration of the faithful departed.
>
> To Jesus Christ, who was, who is, and who is to come, Lord of time and history, be endless praise, for ever and ever.[2]

Several aspects of these practices are worth noting. First, these explicit reckonings of liturgical time are situated within what Barth called the "sphere of the sacrament,"[3] of the Eucharist towards which we are always walking on the way from baptism. While they are part of the commemorations of two major feast days, and outside of what is commonly called ordinary time, they also lie within the ordinary acts of ecclesial life. They are part of the day in, day out and year in, year out round of fast and feast that may seem from the outside to be robustly unproductive. Moreover, the Feast of the Epiphany at which the significant dates of the year to come are pronounced begins the shorter season of ordinary time between Epiphany and Lent. Here, as in the summer version of ordinary time, the usual liturgical color is green, and the season works as a time between the times of feasting at Christmastide and fasting in Lent.

2. Gunn, "Epiphany Proclamation 2020," para. 3.

3. Barth, *Church Dogmatics* I/2, 231.

Second, the two proclamations stand as temporal bookends on the season of Christmastide that cannot be separated from each other. The first marks the incarnation as not merely a metaphor or symbol, but as a particular event that happened in a particular place and at a particular time, once and for all. *Pace* the *Fourth Turning* proponents, the events of Christian time are not available to be co-opted for another project, or to represent a truth behind the truth of the child in the manger. The child in the manger is that truth, irreducibly, and has been born, died, and raised once for all for the life of the world.

At the same time, that event is not merely a point dropped into the middle of the moving staircase of history, not even as the center or focal point of a linear trajectory. The proclamation of Easter at Epiphany, culminating the twelve days of Christmas joy, serves as a double reminder. First, it recalls that incarnation, atonement, resurrection, ascension, and the gift of the Holy Spirit are all bound together within a lifetime of repetition. None of it can be discarded, and none of it can be moved beyond as fitting for one season of either a human lifetime or an historical epoch and not another. Second, it is a reminder that cross and resurrection form the point from which we begin—and from which we begin again. As Christians, we are called to the unproductive repetition of feast and fast, joy and mourning, within which we are always sustained by the body and blood of Christ that sustains us towards the banquet that is yet to come and yet beyond all our reckoning.

It would be tempting to stop here, with the confident announcement of a sacramental reality that is an accomplished work, representing in and of itself a solution to the thorny intellectual and political problems described in the rest of this book. And yet I cannot. The fact that Christians observe the liturgical year has not caused these problems to disappear. No accumulation of eucharistic wafers has prevented practicing Christians from supporting any of the political movements and projects I have named. This work cannot end with a tidy solution, but only with a prayer. Ordinary Christian life in ordinary time, empowered by the Holy Spirit acting in word and sacrament, should call us to a constant work of re-vision and repentance, of comparing the world that is from the world that God has desired for his creatures—and from the world that is yet to come as the new creation. It should call us again and again to our knees, and then to our feet. That is not a matter for academic reflection. It is to be taught, and preached, and lived. May it be so.

Bibliography

Augustine of Hippo. *The Confessions.* Translated by Maria Boulding. New York: Vintage, 1997.

Barth, Karl. *Church Dogmatics.* Translated by G. W. Bromiley, et al. 14 vols. Peabody, MA: Hendrickson, 2010.

———. *Protestant Theology of the Nineteenth Century.* Grand Rapids: Eerdmans, 2002.

———. "A Thank-You and a Bow: Kierkegaard's Reveille." In *Fragments Grave and Gay,* edited by Martin Rumscheidt, 95–101. Translated by Eric Mosbacher. London: Fontana Library, 1971.

Benz, Ernst. *Evolution and Christian Hope.* Translated by Heinz G. Frank. Garden City, NY: Doubleday, 1966.

"Big History Teaching Guide." *Big History Project.* https://school.bighistoryproject.com/media/homepagemedia/CourseGuide.pdf.

Biologos Institute. "The Fullness of Time." August 7, 2011. https://biologos.org/articles/the-fullness-of-time/.

Birney, Ewan. "Why I'm Skeptical about the Idea of Genetically Inherited Trauma." *The Guardian,* September 11, 2015. https://www.theguardian.com/science/blog/2015/sep/11/why-im-sceptical-about-the-idea-of-genetically-inherited-trauma-epigenetics.

Bonhoeffer, Dietrich. *Creation and Fall.* Translated by Douglas Stephen Bax. Dietrich Bonhoeffer Works 3. Minneapolis: Fortress, 1997.

The Book of Common Prayer 1979. New York: Church Hymnal, 1979.

Brody, Richard. "Terrence Malick's Metaphysical Journey into Nature." *The New Yorker,* September 8, 2016. http://www.newyorker.com/culture/richard-brody/terrence-malicks-metaphysical-journey-into-nature.

Brown, Cynthia Stokes. *Big History: From the Big Bang to the Present.* New York: New Press, 2007.

Christian, David. "The Case for 'Big History.'" *Journal of World History* 2 (1991) 223–38.

———. *Maps of Time: An Introduction to Big History.* Berkeley: University of California Press, 2004.

Craig, William Lane. *Time and Eternity: Exploring God's Relationship to Time.* Wheaton, IL: Crossway, 2001.

"Crisscrossing and Connected: Trade, Fuel, and Globalization." *Big History Project.* https://www.bighistoryproject.com/chapters/5#crisscrossing-and-connected.

BIBLIOGRAPHY

Danaher, William. "Renewing the Anglican Moral Vision: What 'Called to Common Mission' Offers Anglican Moral Theology." *Anglican Theological Review* 87 (2005) 63–87.

Daston, Lorraine, and Peter Galison. *Objectivity*. New York: Zone, 2010.

Diamond, Jared. *Collapse: How Societies Choose to Fail or Succeed*. New York: Penguin, 2006.

——. *Guns, Germs, and Steel: The Fates of Human Societies*. New York: Norton, 1999.

——. *The World Until Yesterday: What Can We Learn from Traditional Societies?* New York: Penguin, 2012.

The Episcopal Church in the United States of America. *A Catechism of Creation: An Episcopal Understanding*. 1st ed., revised June 2005. https://episcopalchurch.org/files/CreationCatechism.pdf.

Fabian, Johannes. *Time and the Other: How Anthropology Makes Its Object*. New York: Columbia University Press, 2002.

Ferreira da Silva, Denise. *Toward a Global Idea of Race*. Minneapolis: University of Minnesota Press, 2007.

Fishburn, Janet Forsythe. *The Fatherhood of God and the Victorian Family: The Social Gospel in America*. Philadelphia: Fortress, 1981.

French, Howard W. "E. O. Wilson's Theory of Everything." *The Atlantic*, November 2011. http://www.theatlantic.com/magazine/archive/2011/11/e-o-wilson-rsquo-s-theory-of-everything/8686/.

Ganssle, Gregory E., ed. *God and Time: Four Views*. Downers Grove, IL: InterVarsity, 2001.

Gasman, Daniel. *Haeckel's Monism and the Birth of Fascist Ideology*. New York: Peter Lang, 1998.

——. *The Scientific Origins of National Socialism*. New York: American Elsevier, 1971.

General Assembly of North Carolina. Second Extra Session of 2016. House Bill 2. http://www.ncleg.net/Sessions/2015E2/Bills/House/PDF/H2v1.pdf.

Glarus, Lawrence. "Boldmug Says @Scott Aaronson's Blog." https://lawrenceglarus.wordpress.com/2017/02/12/boldmug-says-scott-aaronsons-blog/.

Gray, Rosie. "Behind the Internet's Anti-Democracy Movement." *The Atlantic*, February 10, 2017. https://www.theatlantic.com/politics/archive/2017/02/behind-the-internets-dark-anti-democracy-movement/516243/.

Gunn, Scott. "The Epiphany Proclamation 2020." *Seven Whole Days*, January 1, 2020. https://www.sevenwholedays.org/2020/01/01/the-epiphany-proclamation-2020/.

Haeckel, Ernst. "Ernst Haeckel Gives Germany's Peace Terms." *The New York Times*, March 19, 1916, 68–69.

——. *The Riddle of the Universe at the Close of the Nineteenth Century*. Translated by Joseph McCabe. New York: Harper, 1900.

Haidt, Jonathan. *The Righteous Mind: Why Good People Are Divided By Politics and Religion*. New York: Vintage, 2012.

——. "Why We Celebrate a Killing." *The New York Times*, May 8, 2011. Section WK, 10. https://www.nytimes.com/2011/05/08/opinion/08haidt.html.

Hale, P. J. "Darwin's Other Bulldog: Charles Kingsley and the Popularization of Evolution in Victorian England." *Science & Education* 21 (2012) 977–1013.

Hall, Amy Laura, and Kara Slade. "The Single Individual in Ordinary Time: Theological Engagements with Sociobiology." *Studies in Christian Ethics* 26 (Feb 2013) 66–82.

Bibliography

Haught, John F. "Big History, Scientific Naturalism, and Christian Hope." In *Creation Stories in Dialogue: The Bible, Science, and Folk Traditions*, edited by Jan G. van der Watt and R. Alan Culpepper, 78–94. Leiden: Brill, 2016.

Hegel, G. W. F. *The Philosophy of History*. Translated by John Sibree. New York: Cosimo Classics, 2007.

Holmer, Paul L. *On Kierkegaard and the Truth*. Edited by David J. Gouwens and Lee C. Barrett. Eugene, OR: Cascade, 2012.

Howe, Neil. "Where Did Steve Bannon Get His Worldview? From My Book." *The Washington Post*, February 24, 2017. https://www.washingtonpost.com/entertainment/books/where-did-steve-bannon-get-his-worldview-from-my-book/2017/02/24/16937f38-f84a-11e6-9845-576c69081518_story.html.

Huntington, Samuel P. *Who Are We? The Challenges to America's National Identity*. New York: Simon & Schuster, 2004.

Immigration Act of March 3, 1903. https://www.loc.gov/law/help/statutes-at-large/57th-congress/session-2/c57s2ch1012.pdf.

Johnson, Elaina, and Eli Stokols. "What Steve Bannon Wants You to Read." *Politico Magazine*, February 7, 2017. http://www.politico.com/magazine/story/2017/02/steve-bannon-books-reading-list-214745.

Kaplan, Amy. "Manifest Domesticity." *American Literature* 70 (1998) 581–606.

Keeley, Louise Carroll. "The Parables of Problem III in Kierkegaard's *Fear and Trembling*." In *International Kierkegaard Commentary Volume 6: Fear and Trembling/Repetition*, edited by Robert L. Perkins, 127–54. 24 vols. Macon, GA: Mercer University Press, 1993.

Kennedy, Maev. "Beware the Time-Eater, Cambridge University's Monstrous New Clock." *The Guardian*, September 18, 2008. https://www.theguardian.com/artanddesign/2008/sep/18/corpus.clock.

Kierkegaard, Søren. *The Concept of Anxiety*. Edited and translated by Reidar Thomte and Albert B. Anderson. Princeton: Princeton University Press, 1980.

———. *Concluding Unscientific Postscript to "Philosophical Fragments"*. Vol. 1. 2 vols. Translated by Howard V. Hong and Edna H. Hong. Princeton: Princeton University Press, 1992.

———. *Either/Or II*. 2 vols. Translated by Howard V. Hong and Edna H. Hong. Princeton: Princeton University Press, 1987.

———. *Fear and Trembling*. Translated by Howard V. Hong and Edna H. Hong. Princeton: Princeton University Press, 1983.

———. *Johannes Climacus*. Translated by Howard V. Hong and Edna H. Hong. Princeton: Princeton University Press, 1985.

———. *Philosophical Fragments*. Translated by Howard V. Hong and Edna H. Hong. Princeton: Princeton University Press, 1985.

———. *Søren Kierkegaard's Journals and Papers*. Vol. 2. 7 vols. Translated by Howard V. Hong, et al. Bloomington: Indiana University Press, 1970.

———. *Works of Love*. Translated by Howard V. Hong and Edna H. Hong. Princeton: Princeton University Press, 1998.

Kiernan, Peter. *Becoming China's Bitch and Nine More Catastrophes We Must Avoid Right Now*. Nashville: Turner, 2012.

Kingsley, Charles. "The Natural Theology of the Future." In *Scientific Lectures and Essays*, 313–36. Works of Charles Kingsley 19. London: Macmillan, 1880.

Land, Nick. *The Dark Enlightenment*. http://www.thedarkenlightenment.com/the-dark-enlightenment-by-nick-land/.

———. "Hyper-Racism." https://alternativerightdotblog.wordpress.com/2014/10/04/hyper-racism/.

Lewis, Ricki. "James Watson on 'Genetic Losers.'" *DNA Science* (blog), December 4, 2014. https://dnascience.plos.org/2014/12/04/james-watson-on-genetic-losers/.

Malick, Terrence, dir. *The Tree of Life*. Toronto: Entertainment One, 2011.

Matthews, Dylan. "The Alt-Right Explained." *Vox*, April 18, 2016. https://www.vox.com/2016/4/18/11434098/alt-right-explained.

McFarland, Ian A. *From Nothing: A Theology of Creation*. Louisville: Westminster John Knox, 2014.

Minus, Paul M. *Walter Rauschenbusch: American Reformer*. New York: Macmillan, 1988.

Moltmann, Jürgen. *The Way of Jesus Christ*. Minneapolis: Fortress, 1980.

Murray, Charles. *Coming Apart: The State of White America, 1960–2010*. New York: Crown Forum, 2010.

O'Connell, Mark. "The Techno-Libertarians Praying for Dystopia." *New York Magazine*, April 30, 2017. http://nymag.com/selectall/2017/04/the-techno-libertarians-praying-for-dystopia.html.

O'Connor, Flannery. *Wise Blood*. 2nd ed. New York: Farrar, Straus and Giroux, 1962.

Peters, Jeremy. "Bannon's Worldview: Dissecting the Message of 'The Fourth Turning.'" *The New York Times*, April 8, 2017. https://www.nytimes.com/2017/04/08/us/politics/bannon-fourth-turning.html

Peters, Ted. "Big History and Big Questions." In *Creation Stories in Dialogue: The Bible, Science, and Folk Traditions*, edited by Jan G. van der Watt and R. Alan Culpepper, 48–77. Leiden: Brill, 2016.

Radner, Ephraim. *A Time to Keep: Theology, Mortality, and the Shape of a Human Life*. Waco, TX: Baylor University Press, 2016.

Ratcliffe, Jonathan. "The Return of the Reactionary (Part II)." *Voegelin View*, January 21, 2017. https://voegelinview.com/rise-reactionary-part-ii/.

Rauschenbusch, Walter. *Christianity and the Social Crisis*. New York: Macmillan, 1920.

Reardon, Jenny. *Race to the Finish: Identity and Governance in an Age of Genomics*. Princeton: Princeton University Press, 2004.

Richards, Robert J. *The Tragic Sense of Life: Ernst Haeckel and the Struggle over Evolutionary Thought*. Chicago: University of Chicago Press, 2008.

"Science and the Big Questions." John M. Templeton Foundation. https://www.templeton.org/what-we-fund/core-funding-areas/science-and-the-big-questions.

Searle, Geoffrey Russell. *The Quest for National Efficiency, 1899–1914: A Study in Politics and Political Thought*. Berkeley: University of California Press, 1971.

Sirvent, Roberto, and Silas Morgan, eds. *Kierkegaard and Political Theology*. Eugene, OR: Pickwick, 2018.

Slade, Kara. "Kierkegaard and the Politics of Time." In *Kierkegaard and Political Theology*, edited by Roberto Sirvent and Silas Morgan, 358–75. Eugene, OR: Pickwick, 2018.

Slattery, John. "Dangerous Tendencies of Cosmic Theology." *Philosophy and Theology* 29 (2017) 69–82.

Stoler, Ann Laura. "Cultivating Bourgeois Bodies and Racial Selves." In *Cultures of Empire: Colonizers in Britain and the Empire in the Nineteenth and Twentieth Centuries*, edited by Catherine Hall, 97–119. New York: Taylor & Francis, 2000.

BIBLIOGRAPHY

———. *Race and the Education of Desire: Foucault's History of Sexuality and the Colonial Order of Things.* Durham: Duke University Press, 1995.

Strauss, William, and Neil Howe. *The Fourth Turning: An American Prophecy.* New York: Broadway, 1997.

Tannenbaum, Frank. "The South Buries Its Anglo-Saxons." *The Century Magazine* (June 1923) 205–15.

Taylor, John C. "The Chronophage." http://www.johnctaylor.com/the-chronophage/.

Teilhard de Chardin, Pierre. *The Future of Man.* Translated by Norman Denny. New York: Harper & Row, 1964.

———. *On Suffering.* New York: Harper & Row, 1974.

———. *The Phenomenon of Man.* Translated by Bernard Wall. New York: Harper & Row, 1959.

Terrall, Mary. "Heroic Narratives of Quest and Discovery." In *The Postcolonial Science and Technology Studies Reader,* edited by Sandra Harding, 84–102. Durham: Duke University Press, 2011.

"To the Civilized World, by Professors of Germany." Reprinted in *The North American Review* 210 (1919) 284–87.

United States Conference of Catholic Bishops. "The Nativity of Our Lord Jesus Christ from the Roman Martyrology." http://www.usccb.org/prayer-and-worship/liturgical-year/christmas/christmas-proclamation.cfm.

Watkin, Julia. "Boom! The Earth Is Round!—On the Impossibility of an Existential System." In *International Kierkegaard Commentary Volume 12: Concluding Unscientific Postscript to "Philosophical Fragments,"* edited by Robert L. Perkins, 95–113. 24 vols. Macon, GA: Mercer University Press, 1997.

Wells, William Charles. *An Account of a Female of the White Race of Mankind, Part of Whose Skin Resembles That of a Negro.* London: Archibald Constable, 1818.

White, Arnold. *Efficiency and Empire.* London: Methuen, 1901.

Wilson, E. O. *Consilience: The Unity of Knowledge.* New York: Vintage, 1998.

———. *The Meaning of Human Existence.* New York: Norton, 2014.

Yarvin, Curtis. "A Gentle Introduction to Unqualified Reservations (Part 9A)." *Unqualified Reservations.* http://unqualified-reservations.blogspot.com/2009/09/gentle-introduction-to-unqualified.html.

———. "Why Carlyle Matters." *Unqualified Reservations.* https://www.unqualified-reservations.org/2009/07/why-carlyle-matters/.

Yehuda, Rachel, et al. "Holocaust Exposure Induced Intergenerational Effects on FKBP5 Methylation." *Biological Psychiatry* 80 (2016) 372–80.

Index

CPSIA information can be obtained
at www.ICGtesting.com
Printed in the USA
LVHW022210291121
704806LV00004B/348